# Lecture Notes in Computer Science 1635

Edited by G. Goos, J. Hartmanis and J. van Leeuwen

## Springer

*Berlin*
*Heidelberg*
*New York*
*Barcelona*
*Hong Kong*
*London*
*Milan*
*Paris*
*Singapore*
*Tokyo*

Xiaoyuan Tu

# Artificial Animals
# for Computer Animation

Biomechanics, Locomotion,
Perception, and Behavior

Springer

Series Editors

Gerhard Goos, Karlsruhe University, Germany
Juris Hartmanis, Cornell University, NY, USA
Jan van Leeuwen, Utrecht University, The Netherlands

Author

Xiaoyuan Tu
Intel Corporation
2200 Mission College Blvd., Santa Clara, CA 95052, USA
URL:http://www.cs.toronto.edu/~tu/

Cataloging-in-Publication data applied for

Die Deutsche Bibliothek – CIP-Einheitsaufnahme

Tu, Xiaoyuan:
Artificial animals for computer animation : biomechanics, locomotion,
 perception, and behavior / Xiaoyuan Tu. - Berlin ; Heidelberg ; New York ;
 Barcelona ; Hong Kong ; London ; Milan ; Paris ; Singapore ; Tokyo : Springer,
 1999
 (Lecture notes in computer science ; 1635)
 ISBN 3-540-66939-6

CR Subject Classification (1998): I.3, I.2.10, H.5.1

ISSN 0302-9743
ISBN 3-540-66939-6 Springer-Verlag Berlin Heidelberg New York

© Springer-Verlag Berlin Heidelberg 1999
Printed in Germany

Typesetting: Camera-ready by author
SPIN: 10703414   06/3142 – 5 4 3 2 1 0    Printed on acid-free paper

# Foreword

After nearly half a century of research, the Holy Grail of the field of artificial intelligence (AI) remains a comprehensive computational model capable of emulating the marvelous abilities of animals, including locomotion, perception, behavior, manipulation, learning, and cognition. The comprehensive modeling of higher animals – humans and other primates – remains elusive. However, the research documented in this monograph achieves nothing less than a functional computer model of certain species of lower animals that are by no means trivial in their complexity.

Reported herein is the 1996 ACM Doctoral Dissertation Award winning work of Xiaoyuan Tu, which she carried out in the Department of Computer Science at the University of Toronto. Tu presents "artificial fishes", a remarkable computational model of familiar marine animals in their natural habitat. Originally conceived in the context of computer graphics, Tu's is to date the only PhD dissertation from this major subfield of computer science (and the only thesis from a Canadian university) to win the coveted ACM award.

Computer graphics addresses the problem of synthesizing images of virtual worlds modeled mathematically on the computer. Computer animation, in particular, is concerned with the computer synthesis of moving images, and it has become an essential technology for the motion picture, advertising, interactive game, and related industries. Over the decades, modeling for computer animation has progressed from an early reliance on purely geometric models to more powerful simulation models that also incorporate physical principles, such as Newtonian mechanics. Tu's pioneering thesis dramatically advances the state of the art by also bringing into play key biological principles. Indeed, her work firmly connects computer animation with artificial life, an emerging discipline which transcends the traditional boundaries of computer science and biological science.

From the perspective of computer animation, Tu's artificial fishes are *not* just highly realistic graphical puppets like the dinosaurs of the landmark feature film *"Jurassic Park"* whose moves were painstakingly plotted by highly skilled human animators. Rather, Tu's models are *self-animating* artificial animals with "eyes" to see their virtual world and "brains" that autonomously govern their actions. They swim, forage, eat, and mate entirely on their own. The significance of her work is that artificial fishes represent not only the geometry and superficial appearance of the animal, as would a traditional computer graphics model. Her sophisticated creations go much deeper to also encompass the function of the animal's muscle-actuated body, sensory organs, and brain. Empowered by artificial life simulations such as Tu's, computer animators can begin to play a role less akin to that of puppeteers and more like that of (National Geographic Society) nature cinematographers, or perhaps some day, like that of motion picture directors of skilled human actors.

This monograph reveals the technical details behind a spectacular accomplishment in computer graphics and artificial life research which has captured mass media attention and has been featured internationally in reputable television programs, news magazines, and newspaper dailies. Readers will see how Tu has interpreted theoretical essentials from biomechanics to perception to ethology and cast them in concrete computational terms within a realistic, computer-simulated virtual world. An important dimension of Tu's work that is not easily conveyed via written document, however, is the beautifully realistic animations of artificial marine ecosystems that are simulated and rendered by her software. Her animations "The Undersea World of Jack Cousto" and "Go Fish!" captured spots in the prestigious computer animation showcase, the *SIGGRAPH Electronic Theater* (1995, 1994). Among other recognition, her animation work received the 1994 *Canadian Academy of Multimedia Arts and Sciences International Digital Media Award for Technical Excellence* and in 1995 it was cited by the computer animation jury of *Prix Ars Electronica*, the premier competition for creative work with digital media.

In my opinion, Tu's work is the most impressive attempt to date towards the elusive dream of AI research that I mentioned earlier. Furthermore, her research (and software) has already helped give impetus to the CS theses of several other graduate students at the University of Toronto, including John Funge's thesis on cognitive modeling for autonomous characters, Radek Grzeszczuk's thesis on learning in artificial animals, Tamer Rabie's thesis on active vision in artificial animals, and Qinxin Yu's thesis on real-time VR. Clearly, Tu's research will continue to have far-reaching implications. Indeed, her artificial fishes have received favorable review from the distinguished evolutionary biologist Richard Dawkins in his bestseller *Climbing Mount Improbable* (Viking, 1996). That a computational model with such interdisciplinary impact can emerge from computer graphics is a testament to the richness and scope of the graphics field today.

As the advisor of Xiaoyuan Tu's thesis, I proudly recommend her book not only to graduate students, computer scientists, and computer animation practitioners, but also to anyone at large interested in computational theories of "how animals work".

*February 1999*                                              *Demetri Terzopoulos*

# Preface

This book develops an artificial life paradigm for computer graphics animation. Animals in their natural habitats have presented a long-standing and difficult challenge to animators. We propose a framework for achieving the intricacy of animal motion and behavior evident in certain natural ecosystems, with minimal animator intervention.

Our approach is to construct artificial animals. We create self-animating, autonomous agents which emulate the realistic appearance, movement, and behavior of individual animals, as well as the patterns of social behavior evident in groups of animals. Our computational models achieve this by capturing the essential characteristics common to all biological creatures – biomechanics, locomotion, perception, and behavior.

To validate our framework, we have implemented a virtual marine world inhabited by a variety of realistic artificial fishes. Each artificial fish is a functional autonomous agent. It has a physics-based, deformable body actuated by internal muscles, sensors such as eyes, and a brain with perception, motor, and behavior control centers. It swims hydrodynamically in simulated water through the controlled coordination of muscle actions. Artificial fishes exhibit a repertoire of behaviors. They explore their habitat in search of food, navigate around obstacles, contend with predators, and engage in courtship rituals to secure mates. Like their natural counterparts, the artificial fishes' behavior is based on their perception of the dynamic environment and their internal motivations.

Since the behavior of the artificial fishes adapts to events in their virtual habitat, their detailed motions need not be keyframed nor scripted. This book therefore demonstrates a powerful approach to computer animation in which the animator plays the role of a nature cinematographer, rather than the more conventional role of a graphical model puppeteer. Our work not only achieves behavioral animation of unprecedented complexity, but it also provides an interesting experimental domain for related research disciplines in which functional, artificial animals can serve as autonomous virtual robots.

## Acknowledgments

Based on a thesis submitted in 1996 to the Graduate Department of Computer Science at the University of Toronto in conformity with the requirements for the degree of Doctor of Philosophy, this book was completed while I was employed at Intel Corporation. The original acknowledgments in the dissertation are reproduced below with minor revisions.

First, I would like to thank my thesis advisors, Professors Demetri Terzopoulos and Eugene Fiume. This thesis would not have been possible without their support.

Demetri has been my mentor in the exciting fields of computer animation and physics-based graphics modeling. His many remarkable qualities have benefited me greatly. I am most impressed by his breadth of knowledge, his ability to seize new ideas, his openmindedness, and his perfectionism towards technical writing. I am especially grateful for the unfailing encouragement he has given me through the years. I would not have come this far this quickly without his expert guidance and the substantial time and effort he put into my thesis.

I thank Eugene for giving me the opportunity to join the graphics group in 1992. Without his kindness and support, I would have been stuck studying operating systems (no offense intended). I appreciate his many insightful comments that have helped to improve my thesis and to put my view into perspective.

My special thanks go to Professor Daniel Thalmann for generously agreeing to serve as external examiner of my thesis, despite his busy schedule and the long distance he had to travel. Special thanks also go to Professor Janet Halperin for serving as internal examiner and Professor Michiel Van de Panne for serving as internal appraiser on my thesis committee. Many thanks to Professors Ken Sevcik and Geoffrey Hinton for serving on my committee and providing valuable comments on my thesis. Special thanks also go to John Funge, for his friendship and support, his consistent encouragement during my thesis research and his assistance in helping to improve my English writing skills.

I thank the wonderful people of the graphics and vision labs. My years at the U of T would have been dull without them. I would like to express my sincere gratitude to Jeremy Cooperstock, Petros Faloutsos, Radek Grzeszczuk, Sherif Ghali, Baining Guo, Beverly Harrison, William Hunt, Joe Laszlo, Michael McCool, Alex Mitchell, Victor Ng, Tamara Stephas, Meng Sun, Jos Stam, Kevin Schlueter, Jeff Tupper, and Corina Xiaohuan Wang from the graphics lab, and Tim McInerney, Victor Lee, and Xuan Ju from the vision lab. My deep appreciation goes to my friends from other groups in the department, Vincent Gogan and Steven Shapiro, and, from elsewhere, Yuxiang Wang, Wei Xu, Tina Shapiro, and Christopher Lori.

I would especially like to thank Michiel Van de Panne who was a student in the graphics lab when I started my PhD program and who now is a professor.

He has always been very generous in helping others around the lab. He taught me how to use the video equipment and provided substantial assistance in the production of my animations. My special thanks go to Radek Grzeszczuk for collaborating in the production of "Cousto", and to Sarah Peebles for producing the sound track for "Go Fish!". Thanks also to John Funge for designing the cover image for this book.

I dedicate this book to my parents, for their endless love and support, for their unwavering confidence in me, and for their limitless patience.

*August 1998*                                                    *Xiaoyuan Tu*

# Contents

# 1. Introduction

*A kangaroo hops across a barren plain. It leaps and lands rhythmically. The harmonic movements of its body, legs and tail trace out graceful curves in the air. A flock of birds glides across the sky. Individual birds flap their wings and adjust their direction autonomously, yet they all fly in unison.*

## 1.1 Motivation

Animals in motion have intrigued computer graphics animators and researchers for several decades. They have long been the subject of study of zoologists and ethologists, and have recently helped inspire the emerging research discipline of artificial life.

In computer graphics, most animations of animals have been created using the traditional and often highly labour intensive keyframing technique, in which computers are employed to interpolate between animator-specified keyframes [1]. More recently, increasingly automated techniques for synthesizing realistic animal motion have drawn much attention. Successful attempts have been made to animate the motions of humans [2, 3], of certain animals [4, 5] and of some imaginary creatures [6, 7, 8]. However, motion synthesis is only part of the challenge of animating animals. Some group behaviors evident in the animal world, such as flocking, schooling and herding [9] have also been simulated and realistically animated in recent feature films.

In this dissertation, we will investigate the problem of producing animation which captures the intricacy of motion and behavior evident in certain natural ecosystems. These animations are intrinsically complex and present a challenge to the computer graphics practitioner. Animations of this sort are of interest not only because they attempt to recreate fascinating natural scenarios, but also because they have broad applicability. They can be used in the entertainment industry, for special effects in movies, for video games, for virtual reality rides; as well as in education as, say, interactive educational tools for teaching biology.

Our goal will be to create the animations that we have described, not by conventional keyframing, but rather through the sophisticated modeling of animals and their habitats. To this end, we have been motivated by and

have contributed to the artificial life (ALife) movement [10]. ALife comple-
ments the traditional analytic approach of biology by aiming to understand
natural life through synthetic, computational means. That is to say, rather
than studying biological phenomena by analyzing living systems, the AL-
ife approach attempts to synthesize artificial systems that behave like living
organisms. An important area of ALife research is the synthesis of artificial animals – or "animats" – implemented both in software and in hardware
[11, 12]. Computational models of simple animals, such as single-cell life forms
[13] and insects [14, 15], have been proposed with interesting results. Many
of these models draw upon theories of animal behavior put forward by ethologists [16, 17].

Since we will view the animation of natural ecosystems as the process
of visualizing computer simulations of animals in their habitats, our work
straddles the boundary between the fields of computer graphics and artificial
life. This theme has also been investigated by Terzopoulos *et al.* [18].

## 1.2 Challenges

Natural ecosystems are as challenging to animate as they are fascinating to
watch. The major challenge comes from their intrinsic complexity. In a given
animation system, there may be a large number of animals, each of which may
exhibit elaborate behaviors. Ideally, one would like to achieve an abundance
of natural intricacy with minimal effort on the part of the animator. The
challenge is exacerbated when one also demands visual authenticity in the
appearance and locomotion of individual animals and in their behavior.

Ecosystems are characterized by the relationships between animals and
their habitats. This means that when we look at an ecosystem, we are keenly
aware of the behaviors exhibited by animals as they interact with their dynamic environment, especially with other animals. For example, a hunting
scenario will not seem authentic if a rabbit hops around carelessly disregard-
ing the presence of a hungry wolf, or if a crowd of pigeons rest calmly while
a child runs in their midst. People's familiarity with various animals imposes
strict criteria for the evaluation of the visual results of our proposed simulations, since even small imperfections in the animated motions or behaviors
will be readily recognizable.

Visual realism, however, is not the only constraint on such animations. For
applications in the entertainment and educational industries, the animator
should be able to control various aspects of an animation. It is especially
important to be able to easily modify an animation; for example, altering
the virtual environment, changing the number, type and distribution of the
virtual animals and, moreover, varying the personalities of the animals and
even interacting with them.

### 1.2.1 Conventional Animation Techniques

Traditional computer animation techniques, such as keyframing, have been used to create many great animations, including those of animals. However, they have several limitations:

**Significant Animator Intervention is Required.** Perhaps the most spectacular instance to date of conventional animation techniques applied to the animation of animals is the dinosaurs in the blockbuster feature film *"Jurassic Park"* (a 1993 Amblin Entertainment Production for Universal Pictures). Yet as realistic looking as they may be, these dinosaurs are merely graphical puppets which require teams of highly skilled human animators to plot their actions and detailed motions carefully from one step to the next. This reveals the main drawback of keyframing: The amount of effort expended by the animator increases dramatically with the length, complexity and intended realism of the animation.

Techniques that do not require as much animator skill, such as motion capture schemes [19], have also been widely used in producing realistic animated motions. However, they tend to be inflexible, since they produce motions that are highly specific, hard to parameterize, and difficult to compose into lengthier animations. Moreover, such schemes are not easily applied to non-human or imaginary creatures.

**Characters Lack Autonomy.** The lack of autonomy of keyframed or motion-data driven characters detracts from the modifiability and inter-actability of the animation. Since realistic behaviors of an animal are subject to the state of its environment (which contains immobile and mobile objects, such as trees, stones, and other animals), slight modifications in a scripted animation, such as moving a tree or adding another animal, may require that the entire animation be re-scripted. Graphical puppets are incapable of actively interacting with their environment. As a result, keyframing techniques are ill-suited to applications such as virtual reality, computer games and interactive educational tools.

**Low-Level Motion Specification is Burdensome.** Using conventional animation techniques, animations are specified at a very low level, thus granting the animator complete control over every aspect of the animation. Complete animator control is sometimes required, especially in cartooning; however, it is generally unnecessary for the sorts of applications in which we are interested. Consider the case of animating a realistic virtual zoo: It is not important if some particular animal appears in some specific posture at some specific time instant; what is important is for the lions and monkeys to look real and for them to move and behave realistically. Complete animator control is also undesirable in our case because it implies little or no autonomy in the animated characters themselves. Therefore, a good strategy for our purposes is to relinquish low-level animator control in favor of a much higher level of control.

**Physical Realism is Not Guaranteed.** Last but not least, using conventional keyframing techniques, realism depends solely upon the skills of the animator. Unless the animator is highly skilled, poor visual results may obtain. In particular, since conventional geometric models possess no mechanical properties, the physical correctness of the resulting motion is not guaranteed, nor will the animated figures respond to forces in a realistic manner.

## 1.3 Methodology: Artificial Life for Computer Animation

### 1.3.1 Criteria and Goals

In light of the preceding discussion, we seek an approach to animating natural ecosystems that is capable of achieving realistic visual effects through an automatic process. The desired properties of such an approach are as follows:

1. The appearance, locomotion and behavior of the animated creatures should be visually convincing.
2. The creatures should have a high degree of autonomy so that this can be achieved with minimal animator intervention. The level of autonomy in the animated animals should, however, permit and support the necessary degree of high-level animator control:
   - The animator should be able to alter the initial conditions of the animation, such as the number and positions of immobile and mobile objects in the virtual habitat.
   - The animator should be able to influence or direct the behaviors of the animated characters to some degree.

The research reported in this thesis develops a highly automatic approach to creating life-like animations and validates it through implementation. Realism is achieved through advanced modeling of animals and their habitats.

### 1.3.2 Artificial Animals

We believe that the best way of achieving our goals in the long run is to pursue the challenging approach of constructing *artificial animals*. The properties and internal control mechanisms of artificial animals should be qualitatively similar to those of their natural counterparts.

There are several properties common to all animals. The most salient one is that *all animals are autonomous*: They have physical bodies that are actuated by muscles, enabling them to locomote; they have eyes and other sensors to actively perceive their environment; they have brains which interpret their perceptions and govern their actions. Indeed, autonomy is the consequence of possessing a brain capable of controlling perception and action in a physical body. The behavior of an animal is a consequence of its autonomous interaction with its environment to satisfy its survival needs. No external control is required for animals to cope with their dynamic habitats, yet their autonomy does not prevent higher animals from being influenced or directed (consider trained circus animals, or human actors).

Artificial animals should be self-animating actors that emulate the autonomy of real animals. In our artificial life approach to computer animation, we build animal-like autonomy into our graphics models; not only to minimize the amount of animator intervention while supporting modifiability and interactability, but also to obtain behavioral realism. Our main concern is how to model the locomotion, perception and behavior capabilities of animals and how to integrate these models effectively within a life-like artificial animal. Our research in this respect shares common goals with ALife research, where artificial animals are often referred to as "animats". Previous animats have been models of simple creatures and the behaviors simulated usually pertain to genetic reproduction and "natural selection" [13, 20]. We attempt to develop artificial life patterned after animals that are more evolved and have a significantly broader range of behavior.

In the following sections, we will identify the essential properties and mechanisms that allow real animals to locomote effectively, to perceive, and hence to behave autonomously. From this we derive design methodologies for achieving realistic animated locomotion and behavior with minimal animator intervention.

### 1.3.3 From Physics to Realistic Locomotion

**Physics-Based Modeling.** The motion of any physical entity is governed at the lowest level by the laws of physics. The use of physics is not new to computer graphics. It was introduced as "physics-based modeling" about a decade ago [21, 22, 23] and has spawned a large body of advanced graphics modeling and animation research. Using physics-based models for graphics not only ensures physical realism of the resulting motion, it also allows subtle yet visually important motions to be animated automatically. Consider, for example, the realistic animation of a stampeding elephant. It would be a heroic chore to try to apply manual keyframing or other purely kinematic methods to animate the rippling flesh, the flapping ears, or the swinging trunk and tail. Physics-based modeling is capable of producing such motions automatically. We will discuss in more detail about physics-based modeling and related previous work in Chapter 2.

**Simulated Physical Body.** The laws of physics and the principles of biomechanics shape the appearance of animal motion. Therefore, the best way to achieve realistic locomotion is to simulate their effects. According to mechanics, the change of the state of an object, or what we commonly call "movement", is caused by forces. The motion of an inanimate object, such as a stone, is generally caused by unbalanced external forces and hence is *passive*. The motion of an animal, on the other hand, is generally initiated by unbalanced internal forces actively generated by its muscles and hence is *active*. Each species of animal has its particular body structure and arrangement of muscles. This in turn dictates its particular mode of locomotion. We therefore construct simulated physical bodies for our artificial animals. By doing so, the laws of physics will guarantee the physical correctness of the resulting motion, while the biomechanical principles relevant to the animal of interest can yield natural muscle actions that simulate the particular locomotion patterns characteristic of the animal in its physical environment.

**Simulated Physical Environment.** The locomotion of an animal not only derives from the dynamics of its body but also is a result of the dynamics of its environment. In accordance with biomechanical principles, various locomotion patterns of animals – e.g. flying, swimming or running – emerge from the interaction between their active muscle-actuated body movements and the reactive physical environment – air, water, or *terra firma*. For example, birds flap their wings inducing aerodynamic forces, which in turn enable them to fly through the air. They cannot fly in a vacuum. Therefore, in addition to modeling the physics of animal bodies, we need also to model the physics of their environments.

**Motor Control.** Upon the computational physics substrate, computed via a dynamic simulation, it is possible to generate realistic locomotion of the artificial animal through simulated muscle control. Through evolution, most natural animals have developed their particular mechanisms for motor control, where coordinated muscle activations result in energy-efficient locomotion. Simulation of effective motor controllers can be derived based on the *a priori* knowledge about the characteristic muscle activations of the corresponding real animal.

### 1.3.4 Realistic Perception

In order to survive in dynamic and often hostile environments, animals are able to adapt their behaviors according to the current situation. As summarized by the ethologist Manning [16], the behavior of an animal "includes all those processes by which the animal senses the external world and the internal state of its body and responds to changes which it perceives." This definition emphasizes the crucial dependence of animal behavior on perception, for without perception, an animal cannot possibly react to its environment. To increase their chances of survival, most animals have evolved acute perceptual modalities, especially eyes, to detect opportunities and dangers in their habitat. The sense organs of animals have specific capabilities and inherent limitations. For example vision is most effective within some proximal distance because, under most circumstances, spatially proximal events will have the greatest effect on an animal. Furthermore, vision is not possible through opaque objects. We must model both the capabilities and the limitations of perception correctly for our artificial animals to exhibit realistic behavior.

### 1.3.5 Realistic Behavior

Given that an animal has the ability to locomote and to sense its environment, its brain is able to interpret the sensory information and select appropriate actions to yield a useful range of behavior.

**Environment, External Stimuli and Internal State.** To enable an artificial animal to behave realistically and autonomously, it is necessary to model relevant aspects of its habitat as well as its internal mental state. Sensory stimuli present information about environmental events such as the presence of food, which may cause the animal to ingest, or the presence of a predator, which may cause the animal to flee. However, external stimuli alone cannot fully determine an animal's behavior. An animal that is satiated will normally not ingest more food even if food is available. If an animal is desperately thirsty, it may delay taking evasive action despite the presence of a predator in the distance in order to drink at a waterhole. Its decision to engage in a particular behavior is predicated on the internal state of the animal which reflects the physical condition of its body – whether it is hungry, tired, etc. Such internal state can thus be considered as inducing the "need" or "motivation" to evoke a specific behavior.

**Action Selection.** After an animal obtains sensory information about its external world and internal state, it has to process this information to decide what to do next. In particular, the perceived external stimuli must be evaluated with respect to the animal's internal state in order for it to determine the most appropriate course of action. This higher control process is often referred to as "action selection". The brain can carry out the action selection process at the cognitive or sub-cognitive level. The action selection mechanism is the key to adaptiveness and autonomy. It is essential to design effective action selection mechanisms for artificial animals.

**Behavioral Animation.** The modeling methodology that we have outlined in the previous sections may be viewed as a sophisticated form of *behavioral animation,* in which autonomous models are built by introducing perception and certain behavioral components into the motion control algorithms [9]. Interestingly, during the last decade, much of the attention in the graphics community has centered on realistic low-level motion synthesis, with only a few researchers pursuing the modeling of realistic behavior. Prior behavioral animation work, however, paid little attention to the realism of the motion of individual creatures. Also, prior work was generally restricted to the animation of one or two specific behaviors and not to the development of broad behavioral repertoires.

### 1.3.6 Fidelity and Efficiency

Our methodology aims at producing autonomous artificial animals that not only look like, but also move like and behave like their natural counterparts. An important question is: How closely should our models attempt to emulate real animals? Clearly, a certain level of modeling fidelity is required in order to generate convincing results and, generally, the more faithful the models, the more realistic the results. Most real animals of interest are extremely complex both in terms of body structure and in terms of behavioral repertoire. Models of animals can therefore easily become excessively complicated. However, it is desirable for an animation system to be reasonably efficient so that it will run quickly enough on current graphics computers to allow interactive modification by the animator.

For the purposes of animation, we must strike a good compromise between model fidelity and computational efficiency. Striking the proper balance is a critical design issue, since inappropriate model accuracy can be counterproductive to the purpose at hand. For example, if we wanted to build a model of a tiger to show the effect of gait on the maturation of the bone in its legs, it may be necessary to model the cellular structure of the bone. However, this is hardly necessary if we are only interested in animating tiger gaits. Therefore we should keep the model complexity as low as is necessary to achieve the intended purpose – in our case, realistic appearance, locomotion and behavior.

## 1.4 Contributions and Results

Fishes[1], the superclass Pisces, are an important species of animals that exhibit elaborate behaviors both as individuals and in groups. Most people find them fascinating to watch. Their behavioral complexity is generally higher than that of most insects, but lower than that of most mammals. Since realistic, automatic animation of the locomotion of humans and other advanced animals remains elusive, a visually convincing virtual marine world presents an excellent choice for validating our approach to animating natural ecosystems.

Imagine a virtual marine world inhabited by a variety of realistic fishes. In the presence of underwater currents, the fishes employ their muscles and fins to swim gracefully around static obstacles and among moving aquatic plants and other fishes. They autonomously explore their dynamic world in search of food. Large, hungry predator fishes stalk smaller prey fishes in the deceptively peaceful habitat. Prey fishes swim around contentedly until the

---

[1] "Fish" is both singular and plural; when plural, it refers to more than one fish *within* the same species. The plural "fishes" is used when two or more species are involved [24].

sight of predators compels them to take evasive action. When a dangerous predator appears in the distance, similar species of prey form schools to improve their chances of survival. As the predator nears a school, the fishes scatter in terror. A chase ensues in which the predator selects victims and consumes them until satiated. Some species of fishes seem untroubled by predators. They find comfortable niches and feed on floating plankton when they get hungry. Driven by healthy libidos, they perform elaborate courtship rituals to secure mates.

We have successfully applied the basic methodology outlined in the previous section to develop an animation framework within whose scope fall all of the above complex patterns of behavior, and many more, without any keyframing. We aim to make the colorfully textured denizens of the fish world as realistic as the "Jurassic Park" dinosaurs. Yet, unlike the dinosaurs, each fish in this community exists as an independent, self-governing virtual agent. None of the actions is keyframed or scripted in advance, but is instead driven by the individual perceptions and internal desires of the artificial fishes. Each fish attends to a hierarchy of needs, with its brain considering the urgency of each situation. When the animation program is initiated, the operator specifies only which fish are present and their initial conditions. Upon starting the artificial life simulation, the creatures proceed to act of their own accord.

The visual results of this work are illustrated by two animations. Our 1993 animation "Go Fish!" [25] shows a colorful variety of artificial fishes foraging in translucent water. A sharp hook on a line descends towards the hungry fishes and attracts them. A hapless fish, the first to bite the bait, is caught and drawn to the surface. The color plates show stills from our 1994 animation "The Undersea World of Jack Cousto" [26]. Fig. 1.1 shows a variety of animated artificial fishes. The reddish fish are engaged in a mating ritual, the large, dark colored fish is a predator hunting for small prey, the remaining fishes are feeding on plankton (white dots). Dynamic seaweeds grow from the ocean bed and sway in the current. In Fig. 1.2, the large male in the foreground is courtship dancing with the female (top). The prey fish in the background are engaging in schooling behavior, a common subterfuge for avoiding predators. Fig. 1.3 shows a shark stalking the school. The detailed motions of the artificial fishes emulate the complexity and unpredictability of movement of their natural counterparts, and this enhances the visual beauty of the animations.

### 1.4.1 Primary Contributions

This thesis contributes both to the field of computer graphics and to the field of artificial life. It leverages the synergy between these two fields for the realistic modeling, simulation, and animation of animals. Our contributions have been published in the computer graphics literature [27, 28] and in the artificial life literature [29, 33].

**Figures 1.1.** Artificial fishes in their physics-based world. See the original color image in Appendix D

**Figures 1.2.** Mating behavior. Female (top) is courted by larger male. See the original color image in Appendix D

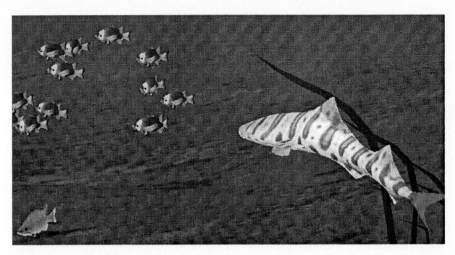

**Figures 1.3.** Predator shark stalking school of prey fish. See the original color image in Appendix D

In computer graphics, this work is the first to combine within a unified framework extensive physics-based graphics models, locomotion control, and higher-level behavioral models for animation. In the context of artificial life, we develop animats of unprecedented realism and sophistication. Our life-like animations of fish in their habitat demonstrate a functional model that captures the interplay of physics, locomotion, perception and behavior in animals. The behaviors that our artificial animals emulate range from reflexive behaviors to motivational behaviors, and from complex individual behaviors to elaborate group behavior. It is important to appreciate that our goal is *not* to attempt to replicate the complete behavioral repertoire of any one specific fish species but, rather, to develop a generic behavioral model suited to the animation of various species of fishes.

The main contributions of this thesis in more detail are as follows:

– We develop an animation framework that, with minimal intervention from the animator, can achieve the intricacy of motion evident in certain natural ecosystems. This framework encompasses realistic appearance, movement, and behavior of individual animals, as well as the patterns of behavior evident in groups of animals. In addition, unlike many other animation systems, our framework has promise for interactive graphical applications, such as virtual reality. Our paradigm is validated by a physics-based, virtual marine world inhabited by a variety of realistic artificial fishes. In particular, we have developed:

1. An efficient, physics-based graphical fish model:
   – We introduce the first graphical fish model to yield life-like aquatic motions without keyframing. Our physics-based fish model captures

the streamlined shape, the muscular structure, and the general biomechanical properties of natural fishes.
- We have constructed a set of motor controllers that effectively control
the muscles of the artificial fish to generate realistic fish locomotion.

2. A perception model: The perception model simulates essential visual abilities and limitations. It is equipped with a perceptual attention mechanism which is lacking in previous perception models for animation. This
perceptual attention mechanism is essential for the realistic modeling of
behavior.

3. A behavior model:
- A model of the internal motivations of an animal which comprises the
innate characteristics of an animal and its dynamic mental state.
- A set of behavior routines that implement a range of individual and
group piscine behaviors that are common across many species, such
as collision avoidance (in the presence of both static and moving obstacles), foraging, wandering, searching for comfortable niches, fleeing,
schooling and mating.
- An "intention generator" that arbitrates among different behaviors
and controls the perceptual attention mechanism.

- This thesis provides a new experimental environment for research in related disciplines, such as computer vision and robotics. For example, artificial fishes have been used to design an active computer vision system and
evaluate its performance [34] and they have been employed to develop algorithms for learning locomotion and other motor skills [37]. Artificial fishes
are virtual robots situated in a continuously dynamic 3D virtual world.
They offer a much broader range of perceptual and animation capabilities,
lower cost, and higher reliability than can be expected from present-day
physical robots used in hardware vision [41]. For at least these reasons,
artificial fishes in their dynamic world can serve as a proving ground for
theories that profess to account for the sensorimotor competence of animals.

### 1.4.2 Auxiliary Technical Contributions

- Interactive tools for capturing the realistic appearance of fishes from pictures:
We have developed a new tool for efficiently obtaining texture boundaries
and coordinates for texture mapping using a deformable mesh.
- A model of a marine environment:
- We model the physical properties of the hydrodynamic medium in order
to simulate its effect on fish motion.
- We have developed a physics-based model of seaweeds that can sway
realistically in simulated water current.
- Numerical algorithms for simulating the biomechanical fish models and their
physics-based environment: The simulator employs an efficient sparse ma-

trix storage scheme and a fast yet numerically stable semi-implicit Euler method.[2]

– A graphical user interface:

- The interface enables the user to create his or her own virtual marine world. For example, the user can decorate the marine environment with static objects and seaweeds, and can specify the number, type, size, initial positions as well as individual habits (i.e. innate behavioral characteristics) of artificial fishes.
- It allows the user to experiment with the physical properties of the fish, the hydrodynamic medium, and the mental parameters of each fish.
- It controls the display of a binocular fish-view from the "eyes" of any chosen fish.

## 1.5  Thesis Overview

The thesis is organized as follows:

In Chapter 2 we review previous work upon which our research draws. At its lowest level of abstraction, our work is an instance of physics-based graphics modeling. Therefore we first survey previous work on physics-based modeling. At a higher level of abstraction, our research is an instance of advanced behavioral animation. We survey prior behavioral animation work and describe related previous perception models developed for the purposes of animation. Then we proceed to discuss the design of action selection mechanisms and review some related previous work in ALife/Animat research.

In subsequent chapters, we describe in detail the animation system that we have developed. In Chapter 3 we begin by presenting a functional overview of the artificial fish model.

In Chapter 4 we describe the biomechanical model and how it achieves muscle-based hydrodynamic locomotion. Next, we develop a numerical simulation of the equations of motion. Subsequently, the motor control of the physics-based artificial fish, derived from piscine biomechanical principles, is presented. This includes the construction of the muscle motor controllers as well as the pectoral fin motor controllers.

Chapter 5 describes our approach to constructing geometric display models that capture the form and appearance of a variety of artificial fishes. An interactive, deformable contour tool is developed and applied to map realistic textures over the fish bodies. Finally we explain how the geometric display models are coupled to the biomechanical fish model to yield realistic animation.

---

[2] It supports the real-time simulation and wire-frame display (30 frames/second) of up to five swimming fish on a Silicon Graphics R4400 Indigo[2] Extreme desktop workstation. If real-time performance is not an issue, a huge number of fish may be simulated and rendered photorealistically on such a system.

In Chapter 6 we present the perception model employed within the artificial fish. In particular, we describe the modeling of the perceptual attention mechanism and the use of motor preferences for generating compromised actions. We present concrete examples of how perception guided behaviors are synthesized. Possible extensions of our perception model are also discussed.

In Chapter 7 we discuss behavior modeling in the artificial fish. We describe the internal motivations and action selection, which is carried out by an intention generator and a set of behavior routines that are explained in detail. Results are presented to illustrate the various behaviors achieved in three varieties of artificial fishes: pacifists, prey, and predators. We then analyze the properties of the action selection mechanism that we have designed and possible extensions are suggested.

Chapter 8 discusses the modeling of the marine environment of the artificial fishes. In particular, we describe the physics-based modeling of seaweeds, food particles and water currents.

In Chapter 9 we present the user interface that we have designed to facilitate the use of our animation system.

In Chapter 10 we describe the animation results that we have achieved to date.

In Chapter 11 we review the contributions of the thesis, and list possible directions of future research.

# 2. Background

In this chapter, we review prior work in the fields of computer graphics and artificial life upon which our research draws. Starting from the lowest level, physics-based graphics modeling, we progressively survey related research on behavioral animation, including perception models for animation and action selection mechanisms. We conclude by putting our work in perspective relative to prior artificial life research on animats.

## 2.1 Physics-Based Modeling

At its lowest level of abstraction, our work is an instance of physics-based graphics modeling. This approach involves constructing dynamic models of animated objects and computing their motions via physical simulation. Physics-based modeling implies that object motions are governed by the laws of physics, which leads to physically realistic animation. Moreover, this approach frees the animator from having to specify many low-level motion details, since motion is synthesized automatically by the physical simulation. This is evident especially when animating passive motion (i.e. motions of inanimate objects) – the animator need only supply the initial state of the object and a physical simulator automatically computes its motion by integrating the differential equations stemming from Newton's laws.

The success of physics-based modeling was demonstrated in modeling the movements of inanimate objects, such as deformable objects [23, 42, 43], chains [44] and tree leaves [45]. A substantial amount of research has also been concerned with the motion of animate objects, such as humans and animals [21, 22, 46, 47].

An animator requires control over physics-based models in order to produce useful animations. We can categorize physics-based control techniques into two approaches: the *constraint-based approach* and the *motion synthesis approach*.

### 2.1.1 Constraint-Based Approach

The constraint-based approach involves the imposition of kinematic constraints on the motions of an animated object [48]. For example, one may constrain the motion trajectories of certain parts of a model to conform to user specified paths. Two techniques have been used to calculate motions that satisfy constraints: the inverse dynamics technique and the constrained optimization technique.

In inverse dynamics, the motion of an animated body is specified by solving the equations of motion. A set of "constraint forces" (or torques) is computed, which causes the animated body to act in accordance with the given constraints [49, 44, 43]. The first two works deal with rigid bodies (for the special case of articulated figures), the third with non-rigid structures. Using inverse dynamics, the resulting motions are physically "correct" (in the sense that the animated body responds to forces in a realistic manner), but they may still look unnatural with respect to any specific form of animal loco-motion. For example, when modeling the locomotion of a cat using inverse dynamics, the resulting motion may not resemble that of a cat, but rather that of a robot. This is because, as was discussed in the previous chapter, an animal's movement not only depends on the Newtonian laws of motion but also is subject to biomechanical principles. In particular, the locomotion of an animal is driven by its muscles, which have limited strength. Therefore, contrary to the assumption of the inverse dynamics technique, a real animal cannot produce arbitrary forces and torques so as to move along any pre-specified path.

The idea behind the constrained optimization technique is to represent motion in the *state-time* space and then define an *objective function* or *performance index* and cast motion control as an optimization problem [6, 50]. The objective function evaluates the resulting motion. The usual assumption is that motions requiring less energy are preferable. An open-loop controller is synthesized by searching for values of the state space trajectory, the forces, and the torques that satisfy the constraints and minimize the objective function. This is usually achieved by numerical methods that iteratively refine a user supplied initial guess and that are often computationally expensive. Moreover, it is possible for the motion to be over-constrained, in which case the optimization algorithm is given the responsibility of arbitrating between the user defined constraints and the constraints induced by the laws of physics [51]. Unfortunately, this means that the compromise solutions produced may not lead to visually realistic motion, especially if the laws of physics are compromised.

### 2.1.2 Motion Synthesis Approach

The motion synthesis approach to physics-based control bears greater resemblance to how real animals move. It synthesizes the muscles in natural animals as a set of actuators that are capable of driving the dynamic model of a character to produce locomotion. Unlike inverse dynamics, the motion synthesis approach can take into account the limitations of natural muscles, and unlike constrained optimization, it guarantees that the laws of physics are never violated. It also allows sensors to be incorporated into the animate models which establishes sensorimotor coupling or closed-loop control. This in turn enables an animated character to automatically cope with the richness of its physical environment. Since this approach can emulate natural muscles as actuators, it is able to synthesize various locomotion modes found in real animals by emulating their muscle control patterns. The quality of the results will of course depend upon the fidelity with which the relevant biomechanical structures are modeled. The motion synthesis approach offers less direct animator control than the constraint-based approach. For example, it is almost impossible to produce motions of an animate body that exactly follow some given trajectory, especially for multi-body models, such as human bodies (though humans do experience difficulty when attempting to produce specific trajectories).

Several researchers have successfully applied the motion synthesis approach to animation [4, 52, 53, 7, 8]. The artificial fish model that we develop is inspired by the surprisingly effective model of snake and worm dynamics proposed by Miller [4] and the face model proposed by Terzopoulos and Waters [52].[1]

An essential physical feature of the bodies of snakes and worms and of human faces is that they are deformable. In both Miller's and Terzopoulos and Waters' works, this feature is efficiently modeled by mass-spring systems. The springs are used to simulate simple muscles that are able to contract by varying their rest lengths. Like these previous models, our fish model is a dynamic mass-spring-damper system with internal contractile muscles that are activated to produce the desired motions. Unlike these previous models, however, we simulate the system using a semi-implicit Euler method which, although computationally more expensive than simple explicit methods, maintains the stability of the simulation over the large dynamic range of forces produced in our simulated aquatic world. Using mass-spring-damper systems, we also model the passive dynamic plants found in the artificial fish habitat.

The major task in motion synthesis is to derive suitable actuator control functions, in particular the time-varying muscle actuator activation functions for different modes of locomotion, such as hopping or flying. When activated according to the corresponding function, each muscle generates forces and torques causing motion of the actuated body parts. The aggregate motion of all body parts forms the particular locomotion pattern. The derivation of actuator control functions becomes increasingly difficult as the number of muscles involved in controlling the locomotion increases. There are two approaches to deriving control functions: the manual construction of controllers and optimization-based controller synthesis, also known as optimal control or learning.

---

[1] An early draft of our model was developed based on a fish model that Caroline Houle (a former student at the graphics lab) built for one of her course projects. I would like to acknowledge her contribution to this work.

**Hand-Crafted Controllers.** The manual construction of controllers involves hand crafting the control functions for a set of muscles. This is often possible when the muscle activation patterns in the corresponding real animal are well known. For example, in Miller's [4] work, the crawling motion of the snake is achieved via a sinusoidal activation (i.e. contraction) function of successive muscle pairs along the body of the snake. Another manually constructed controller for deformable models is that for controlling facial muscles [52, 54] for realistic human facial animation, where a "facial action coding system" coordinates the actions of the major facial muscles to produce meaningful expressions. Most manually constructed controllers have been developed for rigid, articulated figures: Wilhelms [22] developed "Virya" – one of the earliest human figure animation system that incorporates forward and inverse dynamic simulation; Raibert [55] showed how useful parameterized controllers of hoppers, kangaroos, bipeds, and quadrupeds can be achieved by decomposing the problem into a set of manually-manageable control problems; Hodgins *et al.* [47] used similar techniques to animate a variety of human motions associated with athletics; McKenna *et al.* [56] produced a dynamic simulation of a walking cockroach controlled by sets of coupled oscillators; Brooks [57] achieved similar results for a six-legged physical robot; Stewart and Cremer [58] created a dynamic simulation of a biped walking by defining a finite-state machine that adds and removes constraint equations. A good survey of these sorts of approaches can be found in the book by Badler, Barsky and Zeltzer [46].

Fish animation poses control challenges characteristic of highly deformable, muscular bodies, not unlike those of snakes [4]. We have devised a motor control system that achieves muscle-based, hydrodynamic locomotion by simulating the dynamic interactions between the artificial fish's deformable body and its aquatic environment. To derive the muscle control functions for fish locomotion, we have consulted the literature on marine biomechanics [60, 61, 59]. The resulting parameterized controllers harness the hydrodynamic forces on fins to achieve forward locomotion over a range of speeds, to execute turns, and to alter body roll, pitch, and yaw so that the fish can move freely within its 3D virtual world.

The main drawback with manually constructed controllers is that they can be extremely difficult and tedious to derive, especially for many-degree-of-freedom body motions. Moreover, the resulting controllers may not be readily transferable to different models or systems; nevertheless, they can serve as a good starting point for the optimization-based algorithms.

**Optimization-Based Controller Synthesis.** One can also use optimization techniques to derive control functions automatically. An optimization algorithm tries to produce an *optimal controller* through repeated controller and trajectory generation, rewarding better generated motions according to some user specified objective function. This generate-and-test procedure resembles a trial-and-error learning process in humans and animals and is therefore often referred to as "learning". The resulting motion can be influenced indirectly by modifying the objective function. We shall emphasize the difference between the optimization algorithm that we are describing here and the constrained optimization technique mentioned earlier. Here, the laws of physics are not treated as constraints and motion is represented in the *actuator-time* space, rather than in the state-time space.

Since motions are always generated in accordance with the laws of physics, the optimization algorithm is able to exploit the mechanical properties of the physics-based models as well as their environment [51]. Interesting modes of locomotion have been automatically discovered by using simple objective functions that reward low energy expenditure and distance traveled in a fixed time interval [63, 7, 8, 64, 37]. The resulting motions bear a distinct qualitative resemblance to the way that animals with comparable morphologies perform similar locomotion tasks. We shall emphasize, again, that the fidelity of the dynamic model is critical to the realism of the resulting locomotion.

Although we have hand crafted the control functions for the artificial fish's muscles, our model is rich enough to allow such control functions to be obtained automatically through optimization, as is demonstrated by the work of Grzeszczuk and Terzopoulos [37].

## 2.2 Behavioral Animation

At a higher level of abstraction, we are interested in animating the behaviors of animals with an intermediate level of behavioral complexity – somewhere in between the complexity of invertebrates and of primates such as humans. In this regard, our research is an instance of behavioral animation, where the motor actions of characters are controlled by algorithms based on computational models of behavior [65, 9]. Consequently, an animator is able to specify motions at a higher level, i.e. the behavior level, as opposed to specifying motion at the locomotion level as is done in physics-based modeling. The animator is therefore concerned with the modeling of individual behaviors. Behavioral animation approaches have been proposed to cope with the complexity of animating anthropomorphic figures [66], animating the synchronized motions of flocks, schools, or herds [9] and interactive animation control [67].

The seminal work in behavioral animation is that of Reynolds [9]. Creating vivid animations of flocks of birds or schools of fish using conventional keyframing would require a tremendous amount of effort from an animator. This is because, for example, while the overall motion of birds in a flock is highly coordinated, individual birds have distinct trajectories. In keyframing, the animator would have to script each bird's motion carefully in each keyframe. By contrast, Reynolds proposed a computational model of aggregate behavior. In his approach, each animated character, called a "boid", is an independent actor navigating its environment. Each boid has three simple behaviors: *separation, alignment* and *cohesion*. A boid decides which behavior to engage in at any given time based on its perception of the local environmental conditions, primarily the location of neighboring boids. The motions of the individual boids are not scripted; rather, the organized flock is an emergent property of the autonomous interactions between individual boid behaviors.

Although Reynolds' model successfully achieves behavioral realism, it pays little attention to locomotion realism. Because a kinematic model is used to control each boid's locomotion, the resulting motion of individual boids can be visually unrealistic and may not scale well to more elaborate motion. Additionally, the behavioral model is limited by its scope. In particular, since the goal is to animate flocking behavior, each boid is capable by design only of behaviors that are useful to flocking. Our artificial fishes are "self-animating" in the sense of Reynolds' work, but unlike his procedural boid actors, they are more elaborate physical models that also have much broader and more complex behavior repertoires.

### 2.2.1 Perception Modeling

Adaptive behavior is supported by perception of the environment as much as it is by action. It is therefore crucial to model perception in artificial autonomous agents,[2] including animated animals, humans and physical robots. Reynolds' "boids" maintained flock formations through simple perception of other nearby actors [9] while Matarić has demonstrated similar flocking behaviors with physical robots [68]. The roach actor described by McKenna *et al.* [56] retreated when it sensed danger from a virtual hand. Renault *et al.* [69] advocate a more extensive form of synthetic vision for behavioral actors, including the automatic computation of internal spatial maps of the world. The virtual humans in Thalmann's work [70] have simulated simple visual, tactile and auditory sensors that enable them to perform tasks such as following a leader or greeting each other and even playing tennis.

Perception modeling for animation, in general, is very different from that for robotics. On the one hand, in an animation system, the detailed geometry of each scene can always be obtained by interrogating the virtual world model, without extensive sensory information processing. In a robotics system, however, in order for a robot to obtain useful perceptual information, a *visual process* needs to be synthesized. This will include algorithms to infer 3D geometry from images, to identify shapes and to produce appropriate representations of objects, etc. On the other hand, in a typical animation system, since a database of all graphical objects exists and is accessible, the main purpose of modeling perception in animated figures is to enforce behavioral realism. This often only requires that the *perceptual capability* of the

---

[2] An autonomous agent is an entity in a world that can act or behave on it own without explicit external control. Humans and animals are examples of natural autonomous agents.

animal be modeled, such as the field of view and occlusion. Reynolds' model of boids (which only consists of simple modeling of limited field of view) is a good example.

Our artificial fishes are currently able to sense their world through simulated visual perception within a deliberately limited field of view. Subject to the natural limitations of occlusion, they can sense lighting patterns, determine distances to objects, and identify objects by inquiring the world model database. They are also equipped with secondary nonvisual modalities, such as the ability to sense the local virtual water temperature. More importantly, unlike previous perception models for animation, the artificial fish's perception induces an attention mechanism. This mechanism allows the fish to train its sensors in a task-specific way as well as to provide other important information for producing convincing behavior. Our model of perception is proven to be effective in generating realistic behaviors of the artificial fish.

### 2.2.2 Control of Behavior

Behavioral control mechanisms working in conjunction with the perception and the locomotion control mechanisms make our artificial fishes autonomous agents.

To achieve a level of behavioral realism consistent with the locomotional abilities of artificial fishes, it is prudent to consult the ethology literature [71, 72, 73, 74]. Tinbergen's landmark studies of the three-spined stickleback highlight the great diversity of piscine behavior, even within a single species. The artificial fishes' behavior repertoires are modeled after natural piscatorial behaviors common across several species. We achieve the nontrivial patterns of behavior (including schooling behaviors as convincing as those demonstrated by Reynolds) in stages. First, we implement primitive reflexive behaviors, such as obstacle avoidance, that tightly couple perception to action [75, 76]. Then, through an effective action selection mechanism, the primitive behaviors are combined into motivational behaviors whose activation depends also on the artificial fish's mental state, including hunger, libido, and fear.

As the behavioral repertoire broadens, the issue of action selection becomes crucial. In the next section we survey related prior work on the design of action selection mechanisms for autonomous agents.

## 2.3 The Modeling of Action Selection

Designing autonomous agents has been one of the major concerns in several fields of research. In software engineering, intelligent computer programs have been developed that can be viewed as autonomous software agents. These programs automatically accomplish various software tasks with little intervention from the user. In robotics, current research has concentrated on developing autonomous mobile robots that can function successfully with little or no human monitoring. In computer graphics, by modeling each animated character as an autonomous agent, complex animations can be produced with minimal intervention from the animator, as is demonstrated in this thesis.

Any autonomous agent will encounter the problem of action selection. The task of action selection (also known as behavior arbitration or behavioral choice) is to determine, from a set of available actions, the most appropriate one based on the agent's internal and external conditions. Designing effective action selection mechanisms is a major endeavor in the design of autonomous agents. To this end, two questions need to be answered first: "what do we mean by an *action*?" and "what do we mean by *the most appropriate* action?".

### 2.3.1 Defining Action

The term "action" has been used widely in the ethology, psychology and robotics literature, sometimes with quite different meanings. A popular definition of action, in the context of action selection in animals, is given by Tyrrell [77]: an action refers to one of the mutually exclusive entities at the level of *the behavioral final common path* [78]. The level of the behavioral final common path is the lowest level of control in an animal or agent's control system, whereby all behaviors are expressed. However meaningful and accurate from an ethologist's point of view, this definition leads to a certain degree of confusion from a designer's point of view. More precisely, it gives the impression that an action is "a movement", hence the action selection mechanism in an anthropomorphic robot, for example, is responsible for determining the detailed movements of every muscle. As a result, one cannot help wondering how the action selection mechanism is any different from the whole control system of an agent. An alternative is therefore to define an action as a *motor skill*, such as "move forward" or "turn to the right".[3] Depending on the mechanical model of an agent, each of its actions may require a simple single movement of a single actuator or muscle, or a complex series of coordinated movements of a number of actuators.

Defining an action as a motor skill allows us to deal with the problem of action selection at a higher level by differentiating mechanisms for *motor control* from those for action selection. More specifically, given this definition, motor control mechanisms are responsible for controlling and coordinating actuators in an agent so as to form useful motor skills, i.e. actions, while action selection mechanisms are only responsible for choosing an action without knowing how it is implemented. This concept underlies the design of the artificial fish. We first build a motor control system to implement a set of basic motor skills, including swim forward and backward, turn right and left,

---

[3] In fact, although often not explicitly stated, actions are most commonly defined as motor skills in robotics.

glide, yaw, pitch, roll, and brake. The behavior control system is then built to control the selection of these motor skills in order to produce realistic behaviors. Fig. 2.1 illustrates how action selection differs from motor control in a general design scheme. Note that exclusive actions, i.e., actions that use the same actuators/muscles, cannot be selected simultaneously. For example, one can not walk while sitting. However, non-exclusive actions can be selected simultaneously. For example, one can walk while eating.

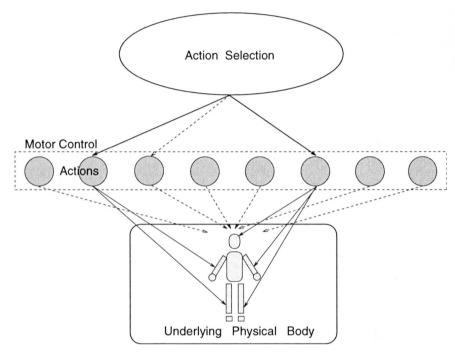

**Figures 2.1.** Differentiating action selection from motor control in design

It should be realized that, currently, motor control in complex animated creatures, such as articulated figures, still remains an unsolved problem. This limits the present feasibility of implementing the above described behavior control scheme in such creatures. However, this should not indicate the lack of generality of the control scheme for we believe that the separation of action selection from motor control is necessary in achieving high level behaviors in most creatures, especially complex ones.

### 2.3.2 Goals and Means

The most appropriate action can be evaluated with respect to the goal of action selection. Animals in the wild often face hazardous situations. The appropriate choice of actions is crucial to their long term survival. Therefore, according to Dawkins [79], the ultimate goal of action selection for animals is to choose successive actions (or behaviors) so as to maximize the number of copies of its genes in future generations. That is to say, the ultimate goal is to survive and to reproduce. This goal breaks down to more immediate, day to day behavioral needs. For a robot, the action selection problem entails maintaining the safety of the robot while pursuing the successful completion of the tasks it has been assigned. For a virtual animal (or an autonomous animated creature in general), the goal of action selection is to achieve satisfactory behavioral realism. Since a mathematical representation of the above goals would be extremely complex, we may not be able to build action selection mechanisms via numerical methods, such as optimization. This makes the problem of deriving action selection mechanisms a design problem and hence the main issue is to come up with the corresponding design criteria [80, 81, 77].

Although the goal of action selection in a real animal seems different from that in a virtual animal, they are in fact similar. The action selection mechanisms in animals allow them to take appropriate actions in the face of uncertainty. This is what we refer to as rational, adaptive behavior. When we say the behavior of a virtual animal looks realistic, we generally mean that the behavior it exhibits makes sense. Like a real animal, the virtual animal "knows" to avoid hazards, to exploit opportunities and to reasonably allocate resources, etc. Our approach to achieving such realism in animation involves identifying the important principles by which animals select actions, especially priorities between different behaviors, and employing these principles as the design criteria for building action selection mechanisms in virtual animals.

### 2.3.3 Previous Work

In prior behavioral animation work, such as that of Reynolds [9], only stimulus-driven action selection process is modeled. For example, the three sub-behaviors of a flocking boid are activated directly by environmental conditions. If the environmental conditions for more than one sub-behavior occur, the weighted sum of the respective responses/actions is taken (each sub-behavior is associated with a weighting factor that reflects its importance). Comparably, Sun and Green [82] specify the action selection of a synthetic actor through a set of "relations" each of which is a mapping from an external stimulus to a response of the actor.

Analogous strategies have been taken in robotics. Representative examples include the rule-based mechanism in "Pengi" developed by Agre and Chapman [83]; and reactive systems and systems with emergent functionality, such as those proposed by Kaelbling [84], Brooks [85] and Anderson [86]. These mechanisms have the main advantage of coping well with contingencies in the environment since actions are more or less directly coupled with external stimuli. However, as Tyrrell [87] points out:

> ... *while we realize that many traditional planning approaches are unsuitable for action selection problems due to their rigidness and disregard of the uncertainty of the environment, we also realize that stimulus-driven mechanisms err in the opposite direction.*

In particular, these mechanisms do not model the agent's internal state thus cannot take into account the agent's motivations. They are therefore limited in dealing with more sophisticated action selection problems faced by agents with multiple high-level (probably motivational) behaviors, such as those faced by most animals.

Being well aware of the aforementioned problems, researchers in ALife and related fields (e.g. robotics) have come up with various implementation schemes for action selection in animats that take into account both internal and external stimuli. This body of work provides valuable reference to our design of the behavior control system of the artificial fish.

Maes [88, 81] proposed a distributed, non-hierarchical implementation of action selection, called a "behavior choice network". The results demonstrate that this model possesses certain properties that are believed to be important to action selection in real animals, such as persistence in behavior, opportunism and satisfactory efficiency. However, while the distributed structure offers good flexibility, it also causes some problems. For example, convergence to a correct choice of behavior is hard to guarantee. Using a similar architecture to that of Maes' network, Beer and Chiel [89] proposed a neuroethology-based implementation of an artificial nervous system for simple action selection in a robot insect.

Along the line of Maes' and Beer's work, others have also proposed various different network-type of action selection mechanisms. For instance, Sahota's [90] mechanism allows behaviors to "bid", and the behavior with the highest bid represents the most appropriate choice.

A common attribute of the above mechanisms (and many others) is the use of a winner-takes-all selection/arbitration process, where the final decision is made exclusively by the winning action or behavior. While this offers highly focussed attention and hence efficiency, it ignores the importance of generating compromised actions. The ability to compromise between different, even conflicting, desires is evident in natural animals. Tyrrell [91] emphasized this particular aspect of animal behavior in the implementation of what is known as *free-flow* hierarchies. A free-flow hierarchy implements compromised actions [92] within a hierarchical action selection architecture similar to those proposed by early ethologists, such as Tinbergen [93]. The winner is only chosen at the very bottom level of the hierarchy. Simulation results [87] show that free-flow hierarchies yield favorable choices of action compared to other mechanisms, such as Maes'. A similar scheme is used to design the brains of the pets in Coderre's [94] *PetWorld*. The main difference between the decision-making (or data-flow) hierarchy in PetWorld and a free-flow hierarchy is that, in the former, sensory data flows from the bottom of the hierarchy to the top while in the latter, it flows top down. The major drawback of such an implementation is its high complexity, hence inefficiency, due to the large amount of computations required.

The behavior system of the artificial fish incorporates both stimulus-driven mechanisms and motivation-based mechanisms for action selection. As a result, the fish possesses a level of behavioral capacity to achieve coherence among a number of complex behaviors. In this regard, our work is compatible with the work by Coderre [94], Maes [88, 81] and Tyrrell [91].

Our implementation is similar to that of Tyrrell in that it employs a top-down hierarchical structure and real valued sensory readings, and it can generate compromised actions. Unlike Tyrrell's model, our mechanism employs essentially a winner-takes-all selection process and allows only certain losing behaviors to influence the execution of the winning behavior. This way action selection is carried out much more efficiently than a free-flow hierarchy. Since more than one behaviors influence the selection of the detailed actions taken for accomplishing the chosen behavior, the final choices of actions are preferable to that generated by a conventional winner-takes-all process. Moreover, the majority of the previous action selection models (including the aforementioned ones) are based on a discrete 2D world which simplifies the problem by greatly restricting legal choice of motor actions. Our model, however, is based on a continuous 3D environment in which the animated animals perform continuous motions.

### 2.3.4 Task-Level Motion Planning

When one attempts to animate advanced animals, such as humans, it becomes necessary to incorporate more abstract action selection mechanisms, such as those based on reasoning. This approach involves using AI techniques and is termed *task-level motion planning* (a good reference book on this subject is the book by Magnenat-Thalmann and Thalmann [2]); The most representative animation work along this line is that by Badler and his group who animated a human figure 'Jack' [95]. The planner takes as input Jack's initial state and a 3D representation of his world and generates as output a series of actions necessary for accomplishing an assigned task, such as "go and get some ice cream".

While planning (or reasoning) ability certainly is one of the most important characteristics in human behavior (and hence is important to model for animations of humans), it is not known as a common feature in most animals lower on the evolutionary ladder than primates. Rather, animal behavior is believed to rest on the more primitive and more fundamental faculty of reactive or adaptive behavior [93, 16, 96]. Adaptive behavior enables animals to be autonomous and to survive in uncertain and dynamic environments. Our approach to behavioral animation reflects the adaptiveness of animal behavior. (Note that we are not referring to adaptiveness in the sense of learning nor evolutionary adaptation, but rather, to the ability to select appropriate behaviors according to the perceived situation.) In our approach, we gain high level control through the construction of a model of adaptive behavior where the actions of an artificial animal result from its *active* interaction with the world as guided by its perception.

## 2.4 Summary

Our approach to developing artificial animals is consistent with the "animat" approach proposed by Wilson [97]. To render our computational model visually convincing, we attempt also to capture, with reasonable fidelity, the appearance and physics of the animal and its world. Artificial fishes may be viewed as animats of high sophistication. They are autonomous virtual robots situated in a continuous, dynamic 3D virtual world. Their functional design, including motor control, perceptual modeling, and behavioral simulation presents hurdles paralleling those encountered in building physical autonomous agents (see, e.g., the compilation by Maes [98]). Previously, the most complex animats were inspired by insects. Brooks (see [57]) describes a physical insect robot "Genghis", bristling with sensors, that can locomote over irregular terrain, while Beer develops a virtual counterpart, a cockroach with simple behaviors in a 2D world [14, 89]. Our work tackles animal behavior more complex than those modeled in existing work such as the above. To deal with the broad behavioral repertoire of fishes, we exploit ideas from physics-based graphics modeling, from biomechanics, from behavioral animation, from autonomous agent studies and from ethology.

# 3. Functional Anatomy of an Artificial Fish

As we discussed in the preceding chapter, there are diverse aspects to the realistic modeling of an artificial animal, from superficial appearance to internal functionality. It is helpful to think of the artificial fish model as consisting of three sub-models:

1. A *graphical display model* that uses geometry and texture mapping to capture the form and appearance of any specific real fish.
2. A *biomechanical model* that captures the physical and anatomical structure of the fish's body, including its muscle actuators, and simulates its deformation and physical dynamics.
3. A *brain model* that is responsible for motor control, perception control and behavior control of the fish.

Each of the three sub-models will be developed in detail in the coming chapters. Fig. 3.1 presents a functional overview of the artificial fish. As the figure illustrates, the body of the fish harbors its brain. The brain itself consists of three control centers: *the motor center, the perception center*, and *the behavior center*. These centers are part of the motor, perception, and behavior control systems of the artificial fish. The function of each of these systems will be previewed next.

## 3.1 Motor System

The motor system comprises the dynamic model of the fish, the actuators, and a set of motor controllers (MCs) which constitutes the motor control center in the artificial fish's brain. Since our goal is to animate an animal realistically and at reasonable computational cost, we have sought to design a mechanical model that represents a good compromise between anatomical consistency, hence realism, and computational efficiency. Our model is rich enough so that we can build motor controllers by gleaning information from the fish biomechanics literature [61, 59]. The motor controllers are parameterized procedures, each of which is dedicated to carrying out a specific motor function, such as "swim forward", "turn left" or "ascend". They translate natural control parameters such as the forward speed, angle of the turn or

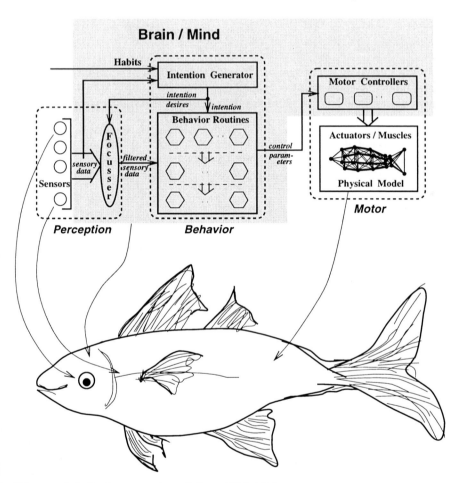

**Figures 3.1.** System overview of the artificial fish

angle of ascent into detailed muscle or pectoral fin actions. The repertoire of motor skills forms the foundation of the artificial fish's functionality.

## 3.2 Perception System

The perception system relies on a set of on-board virtual sensors to provide sensory information about the dynamic environment, including eyes that can produce time-varying retinal images of the environment. The brain's perception control center includes a perceptual attention mechanism which allows the artificial fish to train its sensors at the world in a task-specific way, hence filtering out sensory information superfluous to its current behavioral needs. For example, the artificial fish attends to sensory information about nearby food sources when foraging.

## 3.3 Behavior System

The behavior system of the artificial fish mediates between its perception system and its motor system. An intention generator, the fish's cognitive faculty, harnesses the dynamics of the perception-action cycle. The animator establishes the innate character of the fish through a set of habit parameters that determine whether or not it likes darkness or whether it is a male or female, etc. The intention generator combines the habits with the incoming stream of sensory information to generate dynamic goals for the fish, such as to chase and feed on prey. It ensures that goals have some persistence by exploiting a single-item memory. The intention generator also controls the perceptual attention mechanism to filter out sensory information unnecessary to accomplishing the goal in hand. For example, if the intention is to eat food, then the artificial fish attends to sensory information related to nearby food sources. At every simulation time step, the intention generator activates behavior routines that input the filtered sensory information and compute the appropriate motor control parameters to carry the fish one step closer to fulfilling the current intention. Primitive behavior routines, such as obstacle avoidance, and more sophisticated motivational behavior routines, such as mating, are the building blocks of the behavioral repertoire of the artificial fish.

In the subsequent chapters, we detail the modeling of the aforementioned subsystems of the artificial fish.

# 4. Biomechanical Fish Model and Locomotion

This chapter discusses the motor system of the artificial fish (see Fig. 4.1). In particular, we describe the physics-based fish model and how it achieves locomotion. The biomechanical model we develop is simple, but it is nonetheless effective for realistically animating fish locomotion. We start by presenting the structure of the dynamic fish model, then introduce the dynamics of this model and the simulated aquatic environment. The numerical method employed for solving the differential equations of motion of the fish model is discussed next. Subsequently we describe the biomechanics-based modeling and control of the fish's locomotion, paying special attention to the construction of the motor controllers. This includes the abstraction of the muscle movements for useful locomotion and the functional modeling of the pectoral fins.

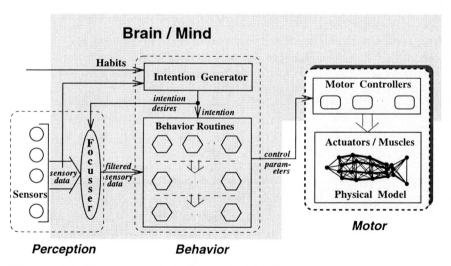

**Figures 4.1.** The motor system of an artificial fish

## 4.1 Discrete Physics-Based Models

The bodies of most fishes are highly deformable structures. We construct our dynamic fish model using a deformable mass-spring-damper system. There are several reasons for this choice:

- A mass-spring-damper model is a simple discrete mechanical structure capable of nonlinear, nonrigid dynamics.
- The spring-damper units in the model are viscoelastic units that serve both as geometric and deformation control primitives.
- Some viscoelastic units may be made actively contractile so that they serve as simple models of muscles.

Both passive and active deformable objects have been successfully animated using similar mass-spring-damper models. Terzopoulos *et al.* [23, 42] developed models for deformable objects capable of exhibiting a range of elastic behaviors. These models effectively animate the nonrigid motions of cloth, paper, metal, rubber, plastic, etc. The active contour models that we employed to compute texture mapping coordinates (see Chapter 5) are also based on such models. Two instances of employing similar mass-spring models for animating active objects are the animation of snakes and worms [4] and the animation of human faces [52, 54].

## 4.2 Structure of the Dynamic Fish Model

Studies of the dynamics of fish locomotion show that most fishes use their caudal fin (i.e. the tail) as the primary motivator [62]. According to Prince [99], there are three main types of caudal propulsion. In the first type, demonstrated by rigid-bodied and armored fish, the tail and a very small part of the adjacent body is used. In the second type, demonstrated by active swimmers such as herring, mackerel, salmon, etc., at least half the body is flexed. In the third type, demonstrated by eels, almost the entire body length is deformed in an undulating action.

We would like to develop the simplest biomechanical fish model whose locomotion synthesizes the second kind of caudal swimming pattern. To this end, we designed a mass-spring-damper model consisting of 23 nodal point masses and 91 spring-damper units illustrated in Fig. 4.2. The units serve as uniaxial deformable elements whose arrangement maintains the structural stability of the body while allowing it to flex. The faces of the nodes are cross-strutted with elements to resist twisting and shearing.

Twelve of the deformable units span the length of the body and serve as simple muscles (the bold lines in Fig. 4.2). These muscles form three muscular segments, each with two pairs of muscles, one on either side of the body. The posterior two segments which cover half of the length of the fish body are used for swimming and the anterior two segments are used for turning. This muscle distribution and usage approximates that found in most natural fish [100].

The shape of a fish directly affects the way it locomotes since the hydrodynamic forces are shape-dependent (more details can be found in Section 4.4). Active natural fishes have evolved a streamlined shape, where their greatest body diameter is just under the midpoint of their bodies [99]. The streamlined shape of the body reduces water turbulence that retards forward motion. The large surface area of the mid-body induces relatively large hydrodynamic forces on the sides which mitigate lateral instability. Since we want the artificial fish to be able to locomote realistically in simulated water, it is important that we design its shape in accordance to the streamlined shape of natural fishes. Fig. 4.3 shows the top and the side view of the physics-based fish model (without the cross-strut viscoelastic units).

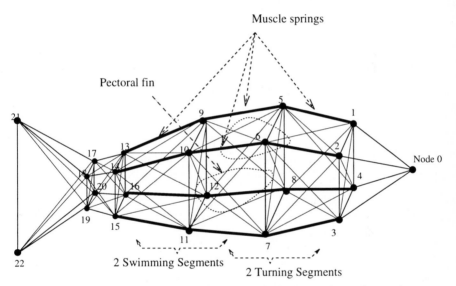

**Figures 4.2.** The biomechanical fish model. Black dots indicate lumped masses. Lines indicate deformable elements at their natural, rest lengths

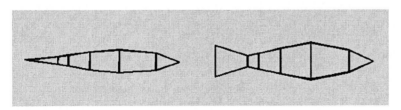

**Figures 4.3.** The top and side view of the outline of the fish model at rest

## 4.3 Mechanics

We will now specify the mechanics of the mass-spring-damper model. Let node $i$ have mass $m_i$, position $\mathbf{x}_i(t) = [x_i(t), y_i(t), z_i(t)]$, velocity $\mathbf{v}_i(t) = d\mathbf{x}_i/dt$, and acceleration $\mathbf{a}_i(t) = d^2\mathbf{x}_i/dt^2$.

### 4.3.1 Viscoelastic Units

Each spring-damper pair forms a uniaxial Voigt viscoelastic unit (Fig. 4.4) that simulates, in a simple way, the viscoelasticity of biological tissue [42]. A Voigt viscoelastic unit comprises an elastic element (a Hookean spring with nonzero rest length) in parallel with a viscous element (a dashpot). Let $S_{ij}$ denote the Voigt viscoelastic unit connecting node $i$ to node $j$. It has elasticity constant $c_{ij}$, viscosity constant $\kappa_{ij}$ and rest length $l_{ij}(t)$ (the rest length of the muscle units may change over time in order to activate motion, see Section 4.6). The deformation of the elastic component is $e_{ij}(t) = r_{ij}(t) - l_{ij}(t)$, where $r_{ij}(t) = ||\mathbf{r}_{ij}(t)||$ and $\mathbf{r}_{ij}(t) = \mathbf{x}_j(t) - \mathbf{x}_i(t)$.

According to Hooke's law, the elastic force that the spring component of $S_{ij}$ exerts on node $i$ is

$$\mathbf{f}_{ij}^e(t) = \frac{c_{ij} e_{ij}(t) \mathbf{r}_{ij}}{r_{ij}}.$$

The same spring also exerts the force $-\mathbf{f}_{ij}^e$ on node $j$.

The linear viscous component of $S_{ij}$ is a dashpot (see Fig. 4.4(b)). It exerts a viscous force $\mathbf{f}_{ij}^v(t)$ on node $i$ which is proportional to $\dot{r}_{ij}(t)$:

$$\mathbf{f}_{ij}^v(t) = \frac{\kappa_{ij} \dot{r}_{ij}(t) \mathbf{r}_{ij}}{r_{ij}}$$

where $\dot{r}_{ij}(t) = (\mathbf{u}_{ij} \cdot \mathbf{r}_{ij})/r_{ij}$ and $\mathbf{u}_{ij}(t) = \mathbf{v}_j(t) - \mathbf{v}_i(t)$ defines the difference between the velocities of node $i$ and $j$. The same component exerts the force $-\mathbf{f}_{ij}^v(t)$ on node $j$.

Given the above derivations of the elastic and viscous component forces, the total force exerted by the viscoelastic unit $S_{ij}$ on node $i$ is

$$\mathbf{f}_{ij}^S(t) = \mathbf{f}_{ij}^e(t) + \mathbf{f}_{ij}^v(t) = \eta_{ij}(t) \mathbf{r}_{ij}(t)$$

where

$$\eta_{ij}(t) = \frac{c_{ij} e_{ij}(t) + \kappa_{ij} \dot{r}_{ij}(t)}{r_{ij}} \tag{4.1}$$

defines the *effective stiffness* of $S_{ij}$.

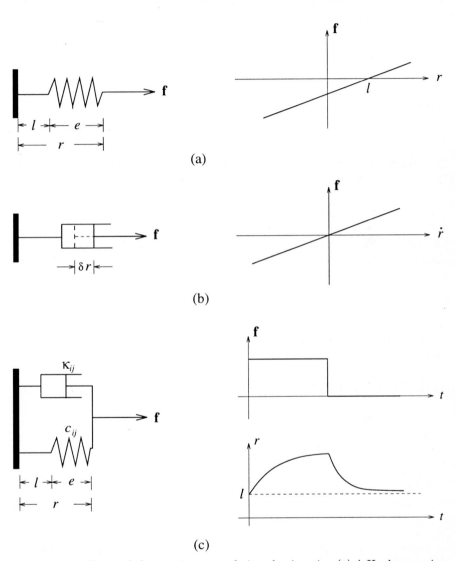

**Figures 4.4.** Uniaxial elastic, viscous, and viscoelastic units. (a) A Hookean spring and its deformation response to applied force **f**; (b) A linear viscous unit and its rate of deformation response $\dot{e}$ to applied force **f**. (c) A Voigt viscoelastic unit and its response to applied force **f**. Adopted from Terzopoulos and Fleischer [42]

**Newtonian equations of motion.** The generalized Newtonian equations of motion governing the dynamic fish model take the form of a set of coupled second-order ordinary differential equations:

$$m_i \ddot{\mathbf{x}}_i(t) + \mathbf{w}_i(t) = \mathbf{f}_i^w(t); \qquad i = 0, ..., 22, \qquad (4.2)$$

where

$$\mathbf{w}_i(t) = -\sum_{j \in N_i} \mathbf{f}_{ij}^S(t) = -\sum_{j \in N_i} \eta_{ij}(t)\mathbf{r}_{ij}$$

is the net internal force on node $i$ due to the viscoelastic units connecting it to nodes $j \in N_i$, where $N_i$ is the index set of neighboring nodes. Finally, $\mathbf{f}_i^w$ is the external (hydrodynamic) force on node $i$.

**Biomechanical Properties.** Efficient locomotion depends on the distribution of the weight and the muscle strength in an animal's body. For example, fish with heavy heads or tails will swim less efficiently and less gracefully than fish with relatively light heads and tails, while fish with either too weak or too stiff muscles will also suffer some degree of motor incompetence. The weight and the muscle strength distributions of the physics-based artificial fish are characterized by the $m_i$ and the $c_{ij}$ of the model, respectively. We set these physical parameters of the model such that the corresponding distributions along the fish body are biologically plausible. For example, the nodes that form the head and the tail of the fish have less mass than those that form the middle part of the body.

The values of parameters used in our simulation are listed in Table 4.1 and Table 4.2.

**Table 4.1.** The mass distribution of the artificial fish. Refer to Fig. 4.2.

| Node $i$ | Attributes |
|---|---|
| $i = 0,\ 13 \le i \le 19$ | $m_i = 1.1$ |
| $1 \le i \le 4,\ 9 \le i \le 12$ | $m_i = 6.6$ |
| $5 \le i \le 8$ | $m_i = 11.0$ |
| $i = 21, 22$ | $m_i = 0.165$ |

Note that the elasticity constants are made large enough to provide the fish's body with the structural integrity that it requires for effective swimming.[1] However, this results in a rather stiff dynamic system that needs a stable numerical solver to simulate its dynamics.

---

[1] More specifically, referring to Table 4.2, the cross viscoelastic units maintain the streamlined integrity of the fish hence have the highest elasticity constants $c_{ij} = 38.0$; The muscles have elasticity constants $c_{ij} = 28.0$, and $c_{ij} = 30.0$ for the remaining viscoelastic units that form other structures, such as the head.

**Table 4.2.** The elasticity and viscosity constants of the artificial fish. Refer to Fig. 4.2.

| Viscoelastic unit $S_{ij}$ | Attributes |
|---|---|
| Cross units, e.g. $S_{27}$ | $c_{ij} = 38.0$ |
| Muscle units: $1 \leq i \leq 12$, $j = i + 4$ | $c_{ij} = 28.0$ |
| Remaining units, e.g. $S_{02}$ | $c_{ij} = 30.0$ |
| All units $S_{ij}$ | $\kappa_{ij} = 0.1$ |

## 4.4 Muscles and Hydrodynamics

An artificial fish moves as a real fish does: by contracting its muscles. If $S_{ij}$ is a muscle, it is contracted by decreasing its rest length $l_{ij}$. The characteristic undulation of the fish tail can be achieved by periodically contracting the swimming segment muscles on one side of the body while relaxing their counterparts on the other side. We will develop the motor controllers that produce this muscle coordination in Section 4.6.

When the fish tail swings, it sets in motion a volume of water. The inertia of the displaced water produces a reaction force normal to the fish's body and proportional to the volume of water displaced per unit time, which propels the fish forward (Fig. 4.5).

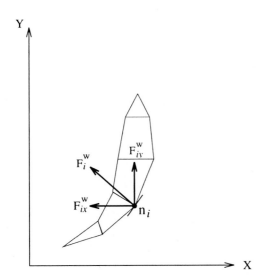

**Figures 4.5.** Hydrodynamic locomotion. With tail swinging towards positive $X$ axis, reaction force $\mathbf{F}_i^w$ at point $n_i$ acts along the inward normal. Component $\mathbf{F}_{ix}^w$ is lateral thrust, while $\mathbf{F}_{iy}^w$ is forward thrust. Aggregate thrust propels fish towards positive $Y$ axis

Assuming irrotational, incompressible and not very viscid fluid, the instantaneous hydrodynamic force on the surface $S$ of a body due to the fluid is approximately proportional to

$$-\int_S ||\mathbf{v}||(\mathbf{n}\cdot\mathbf{v})\mathbf{n}\,dS$$

where $\mathbf{n}$ is the unit outward normal function over the surface and $\mathbf{v}$ is the relative velocity function between the surface and the fluid [101]. For efficiency, we triangulate the faces of the fish model between the nodes. For each triangle, we approximate the hydrodynamic force as

$$\mathbf{f} = \min[0,\ -\mu_w A||\mathbf{v}||(\mathbf{n}\cdot\mathbf{v})\mathbf{n}], \tag{4.3}$$

where $\mu_w$ is the viscosity of the fluid medium, $A$ is the area of the triangle, $\mathbf{n}$ is its normal, and $\mathbf{v}$ is its velocity relative to the water.[2] The external forces $\mathbf{f}_i^w$ (see Eq. 4.2) at each of the three nodes of the triangle are incremented by $\mathbf{f}/3$.

## 4.5 Numerical Solution

To simulate the dynamics of the fish model, the differential equations of motion (4.2) must be integrated over time. The system is intrinsically stiff and can become unstable in a variety of situations that may occur in the simulated dynamic world (e.g. executing a left turn to avoid a sudden dynamic obstacle before completing a right turn). Therefore, the stability of the numerical solution is an important consideration. We employ a simple, numerically stable, semi-implicit Euler method.

The system of equations of motion Eq. (4.2) may be written in the standard matrix form for nonlinear, damped elasto-dynamic systems [102] as follows:

$$\mathbf{M}\ddot{\mathbf{X}}(t) + \mathbf{C}(\mathbf{X})\dot{\mathbf{X}}(t) + \mathbf{K}(\mathbf{X})\mathbf{X}(t) = \mathbf{F}(t) \tag{4.4}$$

where $\mathbf{M}$, $\mathbf{C}$ and $\mathbf{K}$ are the mass, damping and stiffness matrices, respectively. Matrix $\mathbf{M}$ is a constant diagonal matrix with $m_i$ on the main diagonal, while $\mathbf{C}$ and $\mathbf{K}$ are time-dependent nondiagonal matrices. These three matrices are of dimension $n \times n$ where $n$ is the number of nodes in the biomechanical model. Matrices $\mathbf{X}$, $\dot{\mathbf{X}}$, $\ddot{\mathbf{X}}$ consist of nodal position, velocity and acceleration vectors, respectively, and $\mathbf{F}$ is the matrix of external force vectors. These four matrices are of dimension $n \times 3$, such that each row contains the three components of each vector.

Because of the special properties of the viscoelastic units in our dynamic fish system, the damping term $\mathbf{C}(\mathbf{X})\dot{\mathbf{X}}$ and the stiffness term $\mathbf{K}(\mathbf{X})\mathbf{X}$ in the above equation are most conveniently collected into the form of an *effective stiffness matrix* $\mathbf{B}(\mathbf{X},\ \dot{\mathbf{X}})$:

$$\mathbf{B}(\mathbf{X},\ \dot{\mathbf{X}})\mathbf{X}(t) = \mathbf{C}(\mathbf{X})\dot{\mathbf{X}}(t) + \mathbf{K}(\mathbf{X})\mathbf{X}(t)$$

---

[2] We can simulate a fish swimming in fluid of different viscosity up to a certain degree fidelity by changing the value of $\mu_w$. For example, $\mu_w \approx 0$ simulates fish "swimming" in air and $\mu_w > 1$ simulates fish swimming in oil-like fluid.

and hence Eq. (4.4) can be re-written as follows:

$$\mathbf{M}\ddot{\mathbf{X}}(t) + \mathbf{B}(\mathbf{X}, \dot{\mathbf{X}})\mathbf{X}(t) = \mathbf{F}(t) \tag{4.5}$$

where $\mathbf{B}$ is time-dependent since the viscoelastic forces depend nonlinearly on the nodal position and velocity variables $\mathbf{x}_i(t)$ and $\mathbf{v}_i(t)$.

Our method computes the left-hand side of Eq. (4.5) implicitly and the right-hand side explicitly. In particular, we discretize continuous time into time steps, $0, \Delta t, \ldots, t, t + \Delta t, \ldots$ and solve for $\dot{\mathbf{X}}^{t+\Delta t}$ in

$$\mathbf{M}\ddot{\mathbf{X}}^{t+\Delta t} + \mathbf{B}^t\mathbf{X}^{t+\Delta t} = \mathbf{F}^t \tag{4.6}$$

where $t$ represents simulation time and $\Delta t$ is the simulation time step. We do not solve for the position vectors $\mathbf{X}^{t+\Delta t}$ directly because, first, the velocity vectors $\dot{\mathbf{X}}^t$ is readily available since it has to be stored at each time step for computing $\mathbf{B}^t$ (more details can be found in the next section) and, second, using $\dot{\mathbf{X}}^t$ saves us from having to store $\mathbf{X}^{t-\Delta t}$ at each time step. We use the following finite difference approximations for $\mathbf{X}^{t+\Delta t}$ and $\ddot{\mathbf{X}}^{t+\Delta t}$:

$$\mathbf{X}^{t+\Delta t} = \mathbf{X}^t + \Delta t\dot{\mathbf{X}}^{t+\Delta t} \tag{4.7}$$

and

$$\ddot{\mathbf{X}}^{t+\Delta t} = \frac{1}{\Delta t}(\dot{\mathbf{X}}^{t+\Delta t} - \dot{\mathbf{X}}_t) \tag{4.8}$$

Substituting the above equations into Eq. (4.6) and collecting all known vectors on the right-hand side, we obtain a linear system for $\dot{\mathbf{X}}^{t+\Delta t}$:

$$\mathbf{A}^t\dot{\mathbf{X}}^{t+\Delta t} = \mathbf{G}^t \tag{4.9}$$

where

$$\mathbf{A}^t = \Delta t\mathbf{B}^t + \frac{\mathbf{M}}{\Delta t} \tag{4.10}$$

is the effective system matrix and

$$\mathbf{G}^t = \mathbf{F}^t - \mathbf{B}^t\mathbf{X}^t + \frac{\mathbf{M}}{\Delta t}\dot{\mathbf{X}}^t \tag{4.11}$$

is the effective load matrix. As we will explain in the next section, the structure the system matrix $\mathbf{A}^t$ is such that an efficient solution to Eq. (4.9) can be obtained by assembling $\mathbf{A}^t$ and factorizing it as follows:

$$\mathbf{A}^t = \mathbf{LDL}^T, \tag{4.12}$$

where $\mathbf{D}$ is diagonal and $\mathbf{L}$ is lower triangular. The new nodal velocities $\dot{\mathbf{X}}^{t+\Delta t}$ are then computed by first solving the lower triangular system

$$\mathbf{LQ} = \mathbf{G}^t \tag{4.13}$$

for $\mathbf{Q}$ by forward-substitution and finally solving the upper triangular system

$$\mathbf{L}^T\dot{\mathbf{X}}^{t+\Delta t} = \mathbf{D}^{-1}\mathbf{Q} \tag{4.14}$$

for $\dot{\mathbf{X}}^{t+\Delta t}$ by back-substitution. Hence, the numerical simulation of the fish biomechanical model requires the assembly and factorization solution of a sequence of linear systems of the form of Eq. 4.9 for $t = 0, \Delta t, 2\Delta t, \ldots$.

### 4.5.1 System Matrix Assembling and the Skyline Storage Scheme

Since the nodes of the dynamic fish model are not fully connected by viscoelastic units, the effective stiffness matrix $\mathbf{B}^t$ and, consequently (since $\mathbf{M}$ is diagonal), the system matrix $\mathbf{A}^t$, are sparse matrices. Sparsity can be exploited to increase the computational efficiency of the factorization algorithms [103]. We have employed the *Skyline Storage Scheme* for storing $\mathbf{A}^t$, which is popular in numerical methods for finite element analysis [102]. This storage scheme is most efficient for storing sparse matrices that are symmetric and banded. We will now explain our strategy in more detail.

The $n \times n$ system matrix $\mathbf{A}^t$ and $n \times 3$ effective load matrix $\mathbf{G}^t$ are computed according to Eq. (4.10) and Eq. (4.11), respectively. To assemble $\mathbf{A}^t$, we first assemble the instantaneous, internal effective viscoelastic stiffnesses $\eta_{ij}$ of the system (see Eq. (4.1)). Denoting the entries of $\mathbf{A}^t$ as $a_{ij}$ and the rows of $\mathbf{G}^t$ as $\mathbf{g}_i$, the following procedure assembles $\mathbf{A}^t$ and $\mathbf{G}^t$:

1. Initialize $\mathbf{A}^t = \mathbf{0}$ and $\mathbf{G}^t = \mathbf{0}$.
2. For each viscoelastic unit $S_{ij}$, assemble the $\Delta t \mathbf{B}^t$ term of Eq. (4.10) into $\mathbf{A}^t$:

$$a_{ii} = a_{ii} + \eta_{ij}\Delta t$$
$$a_{jj} = a_{jj} + \eta_{ij}\Delta t$$
$$a_{ij} = a_{ji} = -\eta_{ij}\Delta t$$

and assemble the $-\mathbf{B}^t\mathbf{X}^t$ term of Eq. (4.11) into $\mathbf{G}$:

$$\mathbf{g}_i = \mathbf{g}_i + \eta_{ij}\mathbf{r}_{ij}$$
$$\mathbf{g}_j = \mathbf{g}_j - \eta_{ij}\mathbf{r}_{ij}$$

3. Assemble the remaining terms of $\mathbf{A}^t$ and $\mathbf{G}^t$. For $i = 0, \ldots, n$:

$$a_{ii} = a_{ii} + m_i/\Delta t$$
$$\mathbf{g}_i = \mathbf{g}_i + \mathbf{f}_i + (m_i/\Delta t)\mathbf{v}_i$$

Fig. 4.6 shows the structure of the $n \times n$ matrix $\mathbf{A}^t$ which depends solely on the connectivity of the $n = 23$ nodes in the biomechanical fish model. Note that the matrix is symmetric, sparse and banded. Bandedness means that all off-diagonal entries beyond the bandwidth of the matrix are zero. Because $\mathbf{A}^t$ is symmetric, we can state the bandedness condition as

$$a_{ij} = 0, \quad \text{for } j > i + n_{\mathbf{A}} \tag{4.15}$$

where $2n_{\mathbf{A}} + 1$ is the *bandwidth* of $\mathbf{A}^t$ and $n_{\mathbf{A}}$ is called the *half-bandwidth* of $\mathbf{A}^t$. For example, if $n_{\mathbf{A}} = 0$, then $\mathbf{A}^t$ is a diagonal matrix. For our dynamic fish model, $n_{\mathbf{A}} = 7$ (see Fig. 4.6).

The skyline storage scheme exploits the fact that the many zeros outside the skyline of $\mathbf{A}^t$ are unnecessary in the factorization solution of Eq. 4.9. Hence, an effective way of storing the symmetric $\mathbf{A}^t$ would be to store only the

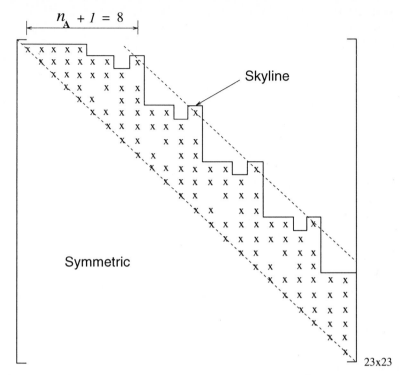

**Figures 4.6.** The structure of the system matrix $\mathbf{A}^t$ of our physics-based fish model, the skyline of $\mathbf{A}^t$ and its half-bandwidth $n_{\mathbf{A}}$. Each "x" represents a non-zero entries

upper triangular half of the matrix below the skyline, including the diagonal.[3] The skyline storage scheme stores $\mathbf{A}^t$ into a one-dimensional array $\bar{A}$. In addition, it uses an auxiliary array to properly address the entries of $\mathbf{A}^t$ stored in $\bar{A}$.

We explain the matrix storage and addressing scheme via a small example system matrix $\mathbf{A}$ of order 4 shown in Fig. 4.7. Let $n_i$ be the row number of the first nonzero entry in column $i$ of $\mathbf{A}$. The variables $n_i$, $i = 0, 1, 2, ...$, define the *skyline* of the matrix and $(i - n_i)$ are the *column heights*. Furthermore, the half-bandwidth of the matrix, $n_{\mathbf{A}}$, equals $\max_i(i - n_i)$. With the column heights defined, we can now store all entries of $\mathbf{A}$ below its skyline consecutively in $\bar{A}$. Fig. 4.7 shows how the entries of $\mathbf{A}$ are stored in $\bar{A}$. In addition to $\bar{A}$, we also define an array $MAX\bar{A}$, which stores the indexes of the diagonal entries of $\mathbf{A}$, $a_{ii}$, in $\bar{A}$. Note that $MAX\bar{A}(i)$ is equal to the sum of column heights up to the $(i-1)$th column plus $i$. Hence, the number of stored entries in the $i$th column of $\mathbf{A}$ is equal to $MAX\bar{A}(i + 1) - MAX\bar{A}(i)$ and the entry

---

[3] Note that zero entries within this region will need to be stored because they can become nonzero during calculations.

indexes are $MAX\bar{A}(i)$, $MAX\bar{A}(i) + 1$, $MAX\bar{A}(i) + 2$, ..., $MAX\bar{A}(i + 1) - 1$. Therefore, storing $\mathbf{A}$ in the form of $\bar{A}$ and $MAX\bar{A}$ allows the entries of $\mathbf{A}$ to be easily addressed.

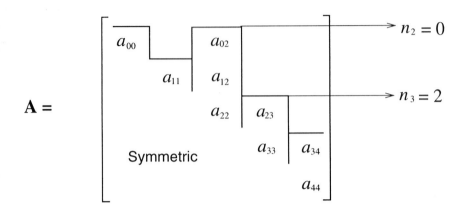

**Figures 4.7.** An example of the skyline storage scheme. $A$ is the example system matrix; $\bar{A}$ is the storage array and $MAX\bar{A}$ is the index array

A factorization solution of Eq. 4.9 using skyline storage is substantially more efficient compared to a Gaussian elimination solution which has $O(n^3)$ complexity in terms of the number of operations required (an operation is defined as a multiplication and an addition), where $n$ is the order of $\mathbf{A}^t$. For factorization with skyline storage, the number of operations required is $O(nn_{\mathbf{A}}^2)$ in the worst case of constant column heights (i.e. $i - n_i = n_{\mathbf{A}}$ for all $i$). Clearly, the larger the difference between $n$ and $n_{\mathbf{A}}$, the greater the advantage. In simulating the dynamics of the artificial fish, we have $n = 23$ and $n_{\mathbf{A}} = 7$ which represents a significant improvement in computational efficiency. Note that the column heights $i - n_i$ of a system matrix $\mathbf{A}^t$ and, hence, the effectiveness of the storage scheme, depends on how the nodes in the discrete dynamic model are numbered. For example, using our current numbering scheme, $n_{\mathbf{A}} = 7$ (Fig. 4.6), however if we number node 22 as node 1 (referring to Fig. 4.2), $n_{\mathbf{A}} = n - 1 = 22$. Thus in general, one should number the nodes in such a way that all connections are as local as possible. We can frequently determine a reasonable nodal point numbering by inspection. However, this numbering may not be particularly easy to generate in certain cases [102].[4]

### 4.5.2 Algorithm Outline and Discussion

An outline of our semi-implicit simulation algorithm is as follows:
  *Initial calculations at $t = 0$:*

1. Initialize $\mathbf{X}^0$, $\dot{\mathbf{X}}^0$ and $\ddot{\mathbf{X}}^0$.
2. From the connectivity of the mass-spring-damper model, initialize the skyline storage scheme: Calculate the dimension of $\bar{A}$ from column heights and the index array $MAX\bar{A}$.

  *For each time step $t = \Delta t, 2\Delta t, \ldots$:*

1. Calculate the system matrix $\mathbf{A}^t$ and the effective load matrix $\mathbf{G}^t$ as prescribed in Section 4.5.1.
2. Factorize $\mathbf{A}^t = \mathbf{LDL}^T$, where $\mathbf{D}$ is diagonal and $\mathbf{L}$ is lower triangular.
3. Solve for the new velocities $\dot{\mathbf{X}}^{t+\Delta t}$:
    a) Solve $\mathbf{LQ} = \mathbf{G}^t$ for $\mathbf{Q}$ using forward-substitution.
    b) Solve $\mathbf{L}^T\dot{\mathbf{X}}^{t+\Delta t} = \mathbf{D}^{-1}\mathbf{Q}$ for $\dot{\mathbf{X}}^{t+\Delta t}$ using back-substitution. Note that since $\mathbf{D}$ is diagonal, the computation of its inverse $\mathbf{D}^{-1}$ is trivial.
4. Update the nodal positions: $\mathbf{X}^{t+\Delta t} = \dot{\mathbf{X}}^{t+\Delta t}\Delta t + \mathbf{X}^t$.

We have verified experimentally that the semi-implicit algorithm is sufficiently stable for our simulation purposes. We use a time step of $\Delta t = 0.055$ in our simulator (the stability limit is reached with a time step around $\Delta t \approx 0.1$). Our algorithm is much more stable than an explicit Euler time integration implementation. Given the same numerical settings, experiments show that the largest time step allowed (before the system becomes unstable) when using our algorithm is typically 100 to 150 times larger than is possible when using the explicit method. On the other hand, our algorithm is simpler than implicit methods described by Bathe and Wilson [102], such as the Houbolt method or the Newmark method. In particular, the approximations we use for

---

[4] The symmetry and bandedness properties of the system matrix associated with the mass-spring-damper fish model would carry over to other mass-spring models [4, 52, 37, 54]. Hence, the skyline storage scheme is generally applicable to these models to improve computational efficiency. Note, however, that all of these prior models used simple, *explicit* time integration methods which do not involve matrix assembly and factorization. As we stated earlier, explicit methods are inadequate to simulate the dynamics of the fish biomechanical model because of their limited stability.

$\mathbf{X}^{t+\Delta t}$ (Eq. 4.7) and $\ddot{\mathbf{X}}^{t+\Delta t}$ (Eq. 4.8) are simple and require only knowledge of the position matrix $\mathbf{X}^t$ and the velocity matrix $\dot{\mathbf{X}}^t$ at time $t$ while other methods (for example the Houbolt method) requires positions and velocities from several previous time steps. Furthermore, fully implicit methods require that the external load matrix $\mathbf{F}^t$ in Eq. (4.6) be calculated implicitly as well, which would be difficult in our case.

## 4.6 Motor Controllers

We have described the structure, mechanics, hydrodynamics and the numerical simulation of the physics-based fish model. In this section, we proceed to describe how we implement the repertoire of biomechanics-based motor skills of the artificial fish.

A critical first step towards higher level, behavioral modeling is to abstract, as a set of motor controllers, the detailed muscle actions, and pectoral fin motions required for locomotion. These motor controllers serve as the behavioral building blocks. They are implemented as parameterized procedures, hence allowing the easy expression of behaviors. In particular, behaviors, as elaborate as the mating behavior, emerge from the invocation of a sequence of motor controllers with appropriate parameters in a meaningful order.

Currently the repertoire of motor skills of the artificial fish is implemented by nine motor controllers:

1. swim-MC
2. left-turn-MC
3. right-turn-MC
4. glide-MC
5. ascend-MC
6. descend-MC
7. balance-MC
8. brake-MC
9. balance-MC

Each motor controller carries out a specific motor function. Four of the motor controllers prescribe the muscle contractions of the biomechanical fish model: swim-MC produces forward caudal locomotion, left-turn-MC and right-turn-MC execute turns, while glide-MC allows gliding and smooth transitions from forward swimming to turning and vise versa. The other five motor controllers control the fish's pectoral fins that enable it to navigate freely in its 3D virtual world: ascend-MC produces lift, descend-MC controls diving, balance-MC enables the fish to maintain its balance, brake-MC slows the forward velocity, and backward-MC allows the fish to retreat.

In the following sections, we explain the implementation of the muscle motor controllers followed by the pectoral fin motor controllers.

### 4.6.1 Muscle Motor Controllers

Muscle motor controllers implement the designated motor functions by controlling the contractions of the twelve muscles.[5] According to Webb [60], given the length of the fish body, the swimming speed of most fishes below certain threshold values is roughly proportional to the amplitude and frequency of the periodic lateral oscillations of the tail. Our experiments with the mechanical model agree well with these observations. Both the swimming speed and the turn angle of the fish model are approximately proportional to the contraction amplitudes and frequencies/rates of the muscles.

The swim-MC (swim-MC(speed) $\mapsto \{r_1, s_1, r_2, s_2\}$) converts a swim speed parameter into contraction amplitude and frequency control parameters for the anterior $(r_1, s_1)$ and posterior $(r_2, s_2)$ swimming segments. One pair of parameters suffice to control each of the two swim segments because of symmetry – the four muscles have identical rest lengths, minimum contraction lengths, elasticity constants, and the relaxations of the muscle pair on opposite sides are exactly out of phase. Moreover, the swim-MC produces periodic muscle contractions in the posterior swim segment that lag $\pi$ radians behind those of the anterior swim segment; hence the mechanical model displays a sinusoidal body shape as the fish swims [60, 61, 104].

For convenience, we define the contraction amplitude control parameters $r_1$ and $r_2$ to be real numbers in the range $(0, 1]$, where 0 corresponds to the muscle's fully contracted length $l_{ij}^c$ and 1 to the muscle's natural rest length $l_{ij}^r$. The frequency control parameters $s_1$ and $s_2$ are expressed as the length of contraction per time step and are in the range $[0, s_{max}]$, where $s_{max}$ represents the maximum frequency ($s_{max} = 0.075$ in our implementation). Through experimentation, we have found a set of four optimal parameters, $\hat{r}_1$, $\hat{s}_1$, $\hat{r}_2$ and $\hat{s}_2$, which produce the fastest swimming speed. The swim-MC generates slower swim speeds by specifying parameters that induce smaller contraction amplitude and frequency than the optimal parameters do. For example, $\{\hat{r}_1, 0.8\hat{s}_1, 1.2\hat{r}_2, \hat{s}_2)\}$ results in a slower-swimming fish. Fig. 4.8a and Fig. 4.8c show snapshots of an artificial fish during caudal swimming motion.[6] Note the resemblance between the shape of the artificial fish during swimming and that of a natural fish during swimming shown in Fig. 4.8b.

Most fishes use their anterior muscles for turning and, up to the limit of the fish's physical strength, the turn angle is approximately proportional to the degree and speed of the anterior bend [60]. The artificial fish turns by contracting and relaxing the muscles of the turning segments (see Fig. 4.2) in a similar fashion. For example, a left turn is achieved by contracting the left side muscles of the segments and relaxing those on the right side at

---

[5] The swimming motor controller controls the swimming segment muscles (see Fig. 4.2), while the turning motor controllers control the turning segment muscles.

[6] The wireframe and shaded fish models shown in Fig. 4.8c will be described in the next chapter.

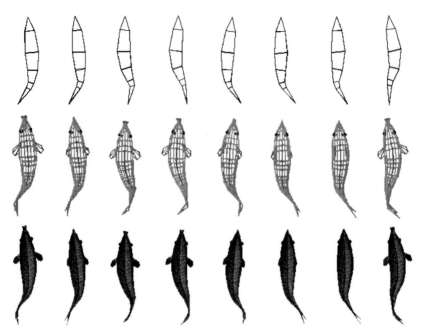

**Figures 4.8a.** Top view of an artificial fish during caudal swimming motion. Note that these snapshots indicate only the shape deformation of the artificial fish during swimming and not the forward motion

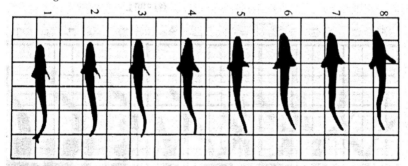

**Figures 4.8b.** Photograph of real fish swimming (reproduced from the book by Blake [61])

**Figures 4.8c.** Top-front view of an artificial fish during caudal swimming motion

a high speed. This effectively subdues the fish's inertia and brings it to the desired orientation. Then the contracted muscles are restored to their natural rest lengths at a slower rate, so that the fish regains its original shape with minimal further change in orientation.

Analogous to the swim motor controller, the left and right turn motor controllers (turn-MC(angle) $\mapsto \{r_0, s_0, r_1, s_1\}$) convert a turn angle to control parameters for the anterior and posterior turning segments to execute the turn (note that the posterior turning segment also serves as the anterior swim segment). Through experimentation, we established 4 sets of parameter values $P_i = \{r_0^i, s_0^i, r_1^i, s_1^i\}$ which enable the fish to execute natural looking turns of approximately 30, 45, 60, and 90 degrees. By interpolating the key parameters, we define a steering map (Fig. 4.9) that allows the fish to generate turns of approximately any angle, up to 90 degrees. Turns greater than 90 degrees are composed of sequential turns of lesser angles. Fig. 4.10 shows the motion of an artificial fish when making a 90-degree turn.

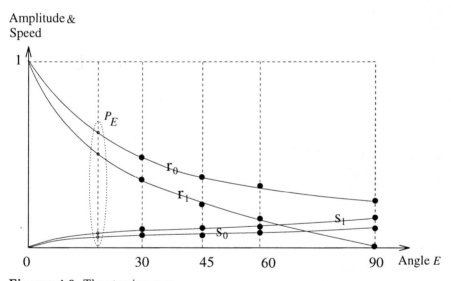

**Figures 4.9.** The steering map

The gliding motor controller (glide-MC($t$)) lets the fish glide through simulated water for up to $t$ time steps. Within the specified time period, all muscles that are not at their natural rest lengths are relaxed to their natural rest lengths so that the fish engages in the next motor function with its original, undeformed shape. The glide-MC induces smooth transitions between the execution of different motor controllers and hence allows the fish to move with the graceful manner of real fish.

**Figures 4.10.** The turning motion of the artificial fish

### 4.6.2 Pectoral Fin Motor Controllers

The pectoral fins on most fish control pitching (up-and-down motion of the body), yawing (the side-to-side motion) and rolling. The pectoral fins can be held close to the body to increase speed by reducing drag, or they can be extended to increase drag and serve as a brake [24]. Many reef fishes use pectoral swimming to achieve very fine motion control, such as backwards motions, by keeping their bodies still and using their pectoral fins like oars. Through functional modeling, we successfully synthesize a full range of pectoral motor control in artificial fishes.

To model the pectoral fins, we equip the artificial fish with five additional parameterized motor skills, namely, the `ascend-MC`, `descend-MC`, `balance-MC`, `brake-MC` and `backward-MC`. The artificial fish is neutrally buoyant in the virtual water and the pair of pectoral fins enable it to navigate freely in its 3D world. The pectoral fins function in a similar, albeit simplified, manner to those of real fishes. For our purposes, the detailed movement of the pectoral fins is of less interest than the movement of the fish body. To simplify the fish model and its numerical solution, we do not simulate the elasticity and dynamics of the pectoral fins. However, we do approximate the dynamic forces that the pectoral fins exert on the body of the fish to control locomotion.

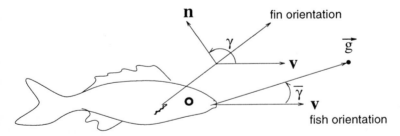

**Figures 4.11.** The pectoral fin geometry

The pectoral fins (Fig. 4.11) work by applying reaction forces to nodes in the midsection of the fish body, i.e. nodes $N_i, 1 \leq i \leq 12$ (see Fig. 4.2). The fins are analogous to the airfoils of an airplane. Pitch and yaw control stems from changing their orientations $\pi/4 \leq \gamma \leq \pi$ relative to the body. Assuming that a fin has an area $A$, surface normal $\mathbf{n}$ and the fish has a velocity $\mathbf{v}$ relative to the water (Fig. 4.11), the fin force is

$$F_f = -A\|\mathbf{v}\|(\mathbf{n} \cdot \mathbf{v})\mathbf{n} = -A(\|\mathbf{v}\|^2 \cos\gamma)\mathbf{n} \qquad (4.16)$$

(cf. Eq. 4.3) and is distributed equally to the 6 midsection nodes on the side of the fin. When the leading edge of a fin is elevated (i.e. $\pi/2 \leq \gamma \leq 3\pi/4$), a lift force is imparted on the body and the fish ascends, and when it is lowered (i.e. $\pi/4 \leq \gamma \leq \pi/2$), a downward force is exerted and the fish descends. When the fin angles differ, the fish yaws and rolls.

The artificial fish can produce a braking effect by angling its fins to decrease its forward speed, i.e. $\gamma = \pi$. This motion control is useful, for instance, in maintaining schooling patterns. As we mentioned earlier, backward swimming motion in natural fishes is usually achieved by backwards oaring of the pectoral fins. In this case, eq. (4.16) is inadequate in producing the control. Nevertheless, for visualization purposes, we do simulate the pectoral oaring motions kinematically (details can be found in Section. 5.5) while producing backward forces proportional to the rowing speed. The combination of the glide-MC($t$) with the backward forces results in the retreating motion useful, for example, during mating behavior.

The parameterization of the pectoral fin motor controllers is simple: The ascend-MC
(ascend-MC($\bar{\gamma}$) $\mapsto$ $\{\gamma\}$) takes the desired angle of ascent $\bar{\gamma} \in [0, \pi/2]$ (see Fig. 4.11) and maps it into the fin orientation $\gamma \in [\pi/2, 3\pi/4]$. Similarly, the descend-MC maps the desired angle of descent into $\gamma \in [\pi/4, \pi/2]$. The balance-MC takes the desired angle of rolling, defined by the angle between the fish's local z-axis $Z_f$ (see Fig. 4.12) and the plane formed by $X_f$ and the world z-axis (pointing upwards), and maps it into two fin orientation angles, one for the left fin and the other for the right fin. The brake-MC takes a constant $\gamma = \pi$ as its parameter and the backward-MC takes the desired speed of retreating and maps it to rowing speed.

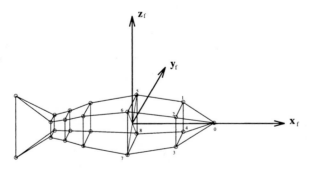

**Figures 4.12.** The local coordinate system of a fish

# 5. Modeling the Form and Appearance of Fishes

To achieve realistic computer animation, our artificial fish model must capture the form and appearance of real fishes with adequate fidelity. In this chapter we design texture mapped, 3D geometric display models with which to "envelope" the biomechanical fish model described in Chapter 4, thus constructing different artificial fishes. We begin with color photographs of real fishes and build free-form geometric models of several different species using nonuniform rational B-spline (NURBS) surfaces. We develop a new interactive tool for segmenting portions of the fish images to be used as texture maps that are subsequently rendered onto the geometric display surfaces. Finally, we describe how this geometric display model is coupled to the dynamic model of the fish to appropriately actuate and deform the display model. We also describe the visualization of the pectoral fin motion in the display model.

**Figures 5.1.** Digital images of real fish

## 5.1 Constructing 3D Geometric Fish Models

The geometric fish models are constructed manually using the $Alias^{TM}$ 3D modeler. We model the shape of any given fish's body in accordance with the shape evident in digitized color pictures of the animal (Fig. 5.1). We employ two juxtaposed NURBS surfaces, one for the left half and the other for the right half of the fish body. The NURBS surfaces are of order 3 (or of degree 4) along both the **u** and **v** axes (**u** and **v** represent the two axes of the material coordinates of a surface). Each NURBS surface has $u \times v$ control points which, when connected, form a surface mesh as shown in Fig. 5.2a. We will refer to this mesh model as the *control-point mesh*. The control points must be updated at each display time step such that the geometric fish model moves and deforms in accordance with the underlying physics-based fish model (the coming Section 5.4 gives the details).

We choose to use a moderate number of control points ($u = 9; v = 21$) for all the geometric fish models in order to achieve satisfactory rendering speed while capturing the characteristic shape of different species of fishes. The NURBS surface generated from the control-point mesh of Fig. 5.2a is shown in Fig. 5.2b.

The dorsal and ventral fins are also NURBS surfaces each of which has $u_1 \times v_1$, $u_1 = 2, v_1 = 12$ control points and is of order 1 along the **u** axis and order 3 along the **v** axis. Note that the lower boundary of the dorsal fin coincides with the upper edge of the fish body and the same relationship holds between the upper boundary of the ventral fin and the lower edge of the fish body. This is achieved by simply making the corresponding control points coincide. The left and right pectoral fins are modeled as polygonal surfaces each with five vertices. Fig. 5.3 shows the geometric fish model with dorsal and ventral fins (top) and with all fins (bottom). Finally, Fig. 5.4 shows the complete geometric models of four different kinds of fishes patterned after the four kinds of natural fishes shown in Fig. 5.1.

## 5.2 Obtaining Texture Coordinates

The next step is to map realistic textures onto the geometric fish display models. The most important step in the texture mapping process is to derive texture coordinates which map the digital image of the real fish onto the 3D surface of the corresponding display model. Once the texture coordinates are determined, the rest of the texture mapping procedure can be carried out via a simple function call in any commercially available 3D graphics software package that supports texture mapping; e.g. $OpenGL^{TM}$, $RenderMan^{TM}$, etc.

Mapping irregular texture images onto irregular 3D geometric shapes is not a trivial problem because the correspondence between the 2D texture coordinates and the 3D object coordinates is difficult to determine automati-

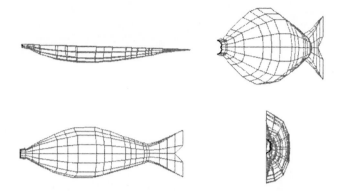

**Figures 5.2a.** Control-point mesh of the left half of a fish body. The perspective view (Top-right); The top view (Top-left); The front view (Bottom-left); The side view (Bottom-right)

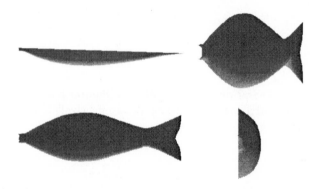

**Figures 5.2b.** The shaded NURBS surface of the left half of a fish body

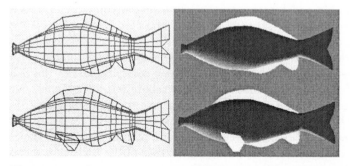

**Figures 5.3.** Geometric model of fish body with fins. The top two images show the control-point mesh (left) and the shaded NURBS surface (right) model with dorsal and ventral fins; The bottom two images show the right-side pectoral fin

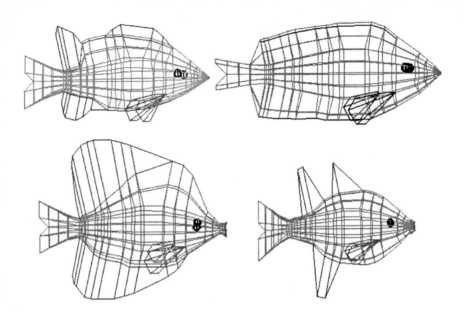

**Figures 5.4.** Control-point mesh fish models

cally. There is currently no general-purpose software to accomplish this task.[1]
In our work, we have developed a new interactive tool for effectively obtaining
texture coordinates from irregular images.

### 5.2.1 Deformable Mesh

Our approach exploits physics-based vision techniques for interactively local-
izing and tracking extended features in images, such as intensity edges. We
employ the active deformable contours (popularly known as "snakes") introduced by Kass, Witkin and Terzopoulos [105]. Deformable contours have been
widely used in reconstructing 2D or 3D shapes from digital image data [106].
We connect a set of deformable contours to form a 2D deformable mesh. To
obtain the texture coordinates for the fish body, we use a deformable mesh
of the same dimension as the control-point mesh covering half of the fish
body (i.e. $9 \times 21$). Similarly, to obtain the texture coordinates for the fins, we
use deformable meshes of the same dimensions as the corresponding control-
point meshes of the fins. A deformable mesh floats freely over an image and
it can be pulled interactively into position using the mouse. Fig. 5.5(a) shows
the initial deformable mesh for capturing the texture of the body of a "strip
emperor" angelfish.

---

[1] Note that this was written in 1995 and the situation may have changed now.

The user begins by interactively dragging the border of the initial, regular deformable mesh such that it comes close to the intensity edges that demarcate the fish from its background in the image. Where necessary, the user may constrain any of the border nodes to selected anchor points on the edges using the mouse. Then the user starts a dynamic simulation that enables the border to approach and conform to the profile of the fish (i.e. the intensity edges) under the influence of an image force field. The remaining contours in the mesh relax elastically to produce a continuous, nonuniform texture map coordinate that covers the imaged fish body (Fig. 5.5(b)). Once the mesh has relaxed, the texture map coordinates are taken as the contour crossing points. In this particular example, since there are no dorsal or ventral fins, the body deformable mesh in fact covers the whole fish image. Appendix A describes in more detail the mathematical formulation of the deformable mesh and how it functions.

(a)                                            (b)

**Figures 5.5.** (a) The initial deformable mesh. (b) The stabilized deformable mesh

## 5.3 Texture-Mapped Models

Fig. 5.6 shows the final texture-mapped geometric fish models obtained from the images in Fig. 5.1. Our animation results reveal that in the artificial fishes application our texture extraction and mapping technique does not suffer much from some of the most typical rendering artifacts encountered in animation of deformable objects, such as 'texture swimming', where parts of the texture slide back and forth on the object's surface.

In conclusion, deformable meshes are an easy to use interactive tool for obtaining texture coordinates that performs well in the mapping of textures from 2D images onto 3D fish shapes. However, the technique could be improved further. A certain degree of texture mismatch is evident by comparing Fig. 5.6 with Fig. 5.1. Fortunately, the mismatch is not detrimental to the realistic appearance of the fishes on the whole. Note that the mismatch is largely due to the fact that the 3D geometric models do not accurately resemble the original fish outline while the deformable mesh does. The problem arises because the process of generating the 3D geometric models is for now separate

**Figures 5.6.** Texture mapped 3D fish models

from that of generating the texture coordinates. With additional work, it should be possible to unify the process of defining the contour control points for the NURBS surfaces with the texture contour generation process.

Another observation is that although texture mapping using scanned digital images leads to photo-realistic appearance, it has several limitations. First, if we want to render a large school of fish of the same species, each with slightly different textures, we would have to store as many digital images as there are fish. Second, many animals, including fishes, may change their colorations during a particular period of time for behavioral purposes. For example, most male fish are able to grow exceptionally colorful textures during mating seasons to attract female fish. Chameleons have the ability to change their colors in accordance with the color of the immediate environment to camouflage themselves. Yet others may change their colors according to their moods. Hence, it may be useful to model the variation of colors and textures across different animals (in the same species) or for any individual animal over time. However it is inconvenient to capture, scan, and segment all the natural images necessary to do so. An alternative approach would be to modify a single captured texture procedurally or to generate purely synthetic textures procedurally. The procedural function that defines the texture (and color) of an animal may depend on multiple factors, such as sizes, identities, currently engaged behavior, environmental colors, and moods of the animal.

## 5.4 Coupling the Dynamic and Display Models

The display models that we have described represent the external surface of the artificial fish's body and give the realistic appearance of a variety of fishes. On the other hand, the dynamic fish model described in Chapter 4, represents the underlying "flesh" that moves and deform over time to produce the locomotion of the fish. The geometric fish surfaces need to be coupled to the dynamic model so that they will move and deform in accordance with the biomechanical simulation. A straightforward way to achieve this task is to associate the control points of the geometric surface model (in this instance, NURBS surfaces) to the faces of the dynamic model.

The dynamic fish model consists of six segments which are denoted as $B_i$, $i = 0, \ldots, 5$. $B_0$ corresponds to the fish's head and $B_5$ the fish's tail (see Fig. 5.7). Each $B_i$ has four quadrilateral faces ($B_0$ and two of the faces of $B_5$ can be treated as quadrilaterals by double counting one of the vertices of the triangles). An intuitive method of associating the NURBS surface to these faces is to find, for each control point of the NURBS surface, a corresponding point on the quadrilateral faces. To this end, we subdivide each face into sixteen patches as shown in Fig. 5.7 and define each face as a parametric bilinear surface with parameters $s \in [0, 1]$ and $t \in [0, 1]$. Let us refer to the 3D vertices of the patches as 'patch-nodes'. After the subdivision, each face has in total twenty-five patch-nodes (four of which are the original vertices that define the corners of the face). Given the values of $s$ and $t$ and the 3D coordinates of the four corners of the face, the coordinates of each patch-node $P(s, t)$ can be easily calculated. The resulting number of patch-nodes covering half of the biomechanical fish model matches the number of control points of the corresponding NURBS surface.

The procedure of obtaining the positions of the control points of the NURBS surfaces over time is as follows:

1. Calculate the positions of all patch-nodes of the initial, undeformed dynamic fish model.
2. Calculate a 3D local coordinate system $(u, v, w)$ for each face. The $u$-axis is the normal of the surface and one of the edges of the face is the $v$-axis.
3. Calculate the "offset vectors" pointing from each patch-node to its matching control point in the local coordinate system.
4. For each display time step:
   a) Update the patch-node positions.
   b) Update the local coordinate systems for each face.
   c) Offset each patch-node by the corresponding offset vector in the appropriate local coordinate system to update the positions of the control points.
   d) Transform the coordinates of control points from the local coordinate systems to the world coordinate system.

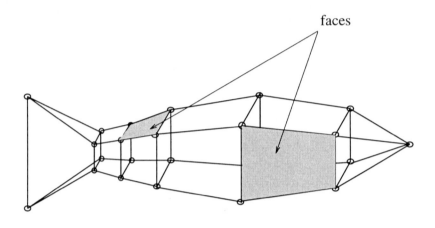

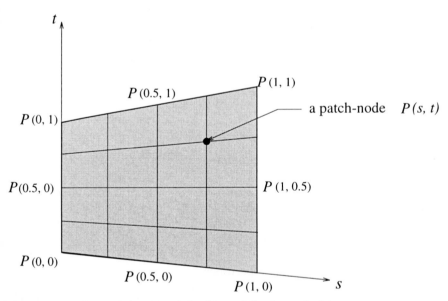

**Figures 5.7.** The subdivision of the faces of the dynamic fish

Fig. 5.8 shows the overlaying control point mesh and the underlying dynamic fish model. Fig. 5.9 shows how the control point mesh deforms according to the shape of the dynamic fish. More importantly, our animations have also demonstrated that unnatural texture distortions due to surface deformation are very small and barely visible.

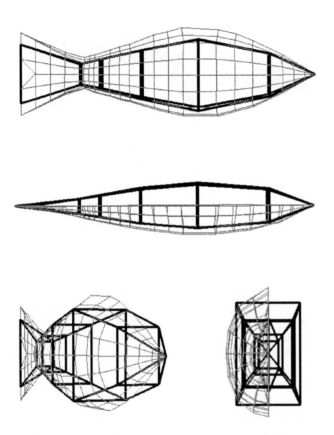

**Figures 5.8.** The geometric mesh surface (half) overlays the dynamic fish model (the dynamic model does not show all the viscoelastic units)

## 5.5 Visualization of the Pectoral Motions

Visualizing the motion of the pectoral fins is important for enhancing the authentic quality of the artificial fish model. A pair of motionless pectoral fins can make an otherwise life-like swimming fish look awkward. From the

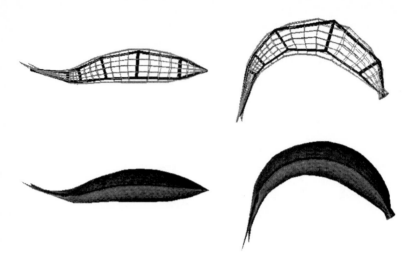

**Figures 5.9.** The geometric NURBS surface fish deforms with the dynamic fish

simplified functional modeling of the pectoral fins described in Section 4.6.2, a straightforward visualization will be to make the geometric model of the pectoral fins be at an angle corresponding to the $\gamma$'s. Since $\gamma$ will only change when necessary and successive $\gamma$ angles are generally not continuous, the fin motion will unfortunately look sudden, stiff and hence unrealistic. If we interpolate the angles to yield smooth motion, the fins will look almost motionless compared to the fish's lively body movement. For this reason, we separate the control for visualization purpose from the control for fish locomotion (or functional purpose) described in Chapter 4.

Real fish can move their pectoral fins in extremely subtle and complex ways that may not be possible to capture accurately using our simplified model. However, many of these delicate details of the fin motions are barely detectable from any distance. In fact, the pectoral fins often move so quickly that only a rough motion pattern, such as flapping or oaring, is distinguishable. We have simulated these two main motion patterns of pectoral movement in the artificial fishes. The implementation details can be found in Appendix B and the results are depicted in Fig. 5.10 and Fig. 5.11 below.

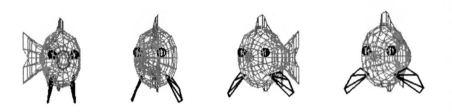

**Figures 5.10.** Snapshots of the pectoral flapping motion

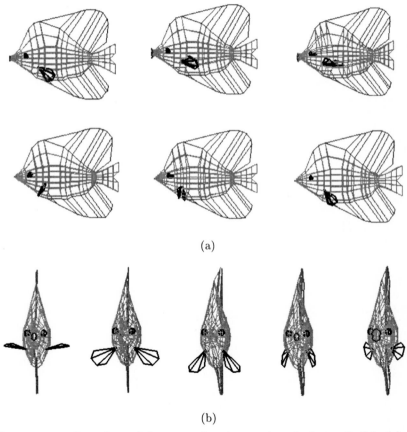

(a)

(b)

**Figures 5.11.** Snapshots of the pectoral oaring motion of a butterfly fish: (a) side view (b) front view

# 6. Perception Modeling

Perception is at least as crucial a characteristic of animals as is locomotion, for an animal must perceive its environment in order to survive. Different kinds of animals usually have different perceptual organs specialized to their particular habitats. Some animals live in the air more than upon the ground; some prefer bright light while others tend to live more or less in darkness. The faculties of sense organs can be determined, with relative ease, by studying their structures. However, it is hard to ascertain how animals actually interpret perceptual information – even for those animals with rather simple sense organs, perceptual processes are diverse and complex [107]. For example, birds are known to recognize their mates by the coloration of their feathers, but when such features are absent they are still able to recognize mates by studying the behavior and the dancing and posturing which may be associated with courtship.

## 6.1 Perception Modeling for Animation

Perception modeling for animation is concerned with:

1. Simulating the physical and optical abilities and limitations of the animal's perception.
2. Interpreting sensory data by simulating the results of perceptual information processing within the brain of the animal.

When modeling perception for the purposes of animation, our first task is to model the perceptual capabilities of the animal. Many animals employ eyes as their primary sense organ and perceptual information is extracted from retinal images. In an animation system, such "retinal" images correspond to the 2D projection of the 3D virtual world rendered from the point of view of the artificial animal's "eyes". However, many animals do not rely on vision as their primary perceptual mode, in which case vision models alone may not be able to appropriately capture the animal's perceptual abilities.

It is equally important to model the limitations of natural perception. Animal sensory organs cannot provide unlimited information about their habitats. Most animals cannot detect objects that are beyond a certain distance away and they usually can detect moving objects much better than static objects [108]. If these properties are not adequately modeled, unrealistic behaviors may result.

Moreover, at any moment in time, an animal receives a relatively large amount of sensory information to which its brain cannot attend all at once. Hence there must be some mechanism for deciding what particular information to attend to at any particular time. This process is often referred to as *attention*. The focus of attention is determined based upon the animal's behavioral needs and is a crucial part of perception that directly connects perception to behavior.

Unfortunately, it is not at all well understood how to model animal sensory organs, let alone the information processing in the brain that mediate an animal's perception of its world. Fortunately, for the purposes of animation, an artificial animal in its virtual world can readily glean whatever sensory information is necessary to support life-like behavior by directly interrogating the world model and/or exploiting the graphics rendering pipeline. In this way, our perception model synthesizes the *results* of perception in as simple, direct and efficient a manner as possible.

## 6.2 Overview of the Artificial Fish's Perception System

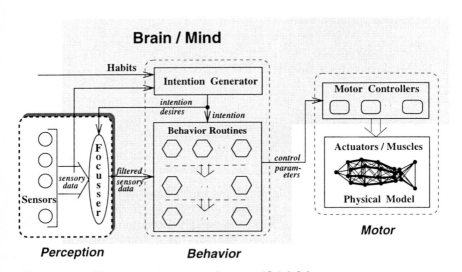

**Figures 6.1.** The perception system in an artificial fish

The perception system of the artificial fish, illustrated in Fig. 6.1, comprises a set of virtual on-board sensors and a perceptual focusser. Currently the artificial fish is equipped with two sensors that provide information about the dynamic environment – a temperature sensor that measures the ambient (virtual) water temperature at the center of the artificial fish's body and a vision sensor. The focusser is a perceptual attention mechanism which allows the artificial fish to train its sensors at the world in a task-specific way, hence filtering out sensory information superfluous to the needs of the engaged behavior. In the remainder of this chapter, we describe in detail our implementation of the perceptual mechanisms of the artificial fish and show how perception governs some of the most critical behaviors (i.e. reflexive behavior).

## 6.3 Vision Sensor Modeling

The vision sensor of the artificial fish functions mainly as the eyes and/or the body lateral lines that enable it to detect objects in the environment that are relevant to its survival, such as food, predators, and mates. Artificial fishes also incorporate other sensing abilities observed in natural fish, such as olfactory sensing, which are essential for effective foraging. For example, predator fish, such as sharks, can stalk prey in murky water by detecting their chemical scent in the water.

### 6.3.1 Perceptual Range

As we stated in the beginning of this chapter, it is also important to model the basic limitations of animal perception systems. The cyclopean vision sensor is limited to a 300 degree spherical angle extending to an effective radius $V_r$ that is appropriate for the visibility of the translucent water. The spherical angle and the visual range $V_r$ define a view volume within which objects can be seen.[1]

As we mentioned earlier, many animals in the wild possess special sensing abilities for tracking food. We model additional perceptual clues which are isotropic, such as olfactory perception (i.e. sense of smell), by expanding $V_r$ to a larger radius $O_r$. The strengthened perceptual ability allows our artificial fish to perceive food (but not other objects) within a certain distance, even if it is out of sight. Another purpose of modeling this additional food-sensing ability is to make foraging behavior more interesting. Imagine a fish feeding on floating plankton. Due to the water current the plankton it is after may drift out of sight temporarily. Instead of forgetting about the food it had just seen and chased, the sense of smell enables the fish to continue the pursuit. Fig. 6.2 illustrates the perceptual range.

The radius of the view volume $V_r$ should be influenced by the size of the object. An object of normal size in the distance may be too far to be seen, but this may not be the case if a much larger object is placed at the same

---

[1] In our case, one can view the modeling of perceptual range as restricting the 'visible' portion of the graphics database of the scene.

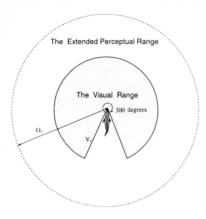

**Figures 6.2.** Vision sensor. Visual perception is limited to 300 degree solid angle and radius $V_r$ (view volume), while the extended perceptual range is limited to radius $O_r > V_r$

distance. It is especially important to model this effect such that small prey fish can detect the presence of large predator fish well in advance. To this end, we associate a 'size parameter' $s_i^p$ with each fish $i$ in the animation. $s_i^p = 1$ represents the *standard* size, while $s_i^p > 1$ represents larger sizes. When $V_r$ is used for determining whether fish $i$ is visible, $V_r$ is scaled by the size parameter $s_i^p$ (example can be found in Section 6.4.2).

### 6.3.2 Occlusion

Another limitation of natural vision is occlusion. Occlusion is also modeled in the visual perception of the artificial fish (see Fig. 6.3). An object is "seen" if and only if some part of it enters the visual range (or view volume) and it is not fully occluded behind some other opaque object. Implementation details will be described in the next section.

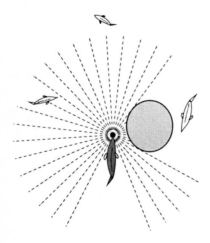

**Figures 6.3.** Occlusion and distance limit the visual perception of objects (only the fish to the left is visible)

### 6.3.3 Functionality

As we have indicated earlier, the artificial fish's vision sensor has access to the geometry, material property, and illumination information about the world that is available to the graphics pipeline for rendering purposes. In addition, the vision sensor can interrogate the world model database to identify nearby objects and interrogate the physical simulation to obtain information such as the instantaneous positions and velocities of objects of interest. In this way, the vision sensor extracts from the 3D virtual world only some of the most useful information that piscine visual processes can provide real fishes about their world, such as the colors, sizes, distances, and identities of visible objects.

A basic item of information in terms of the artificial fish's behavioral repertoire is the overall brightness of the environment, which is obtained as the mean intensity of the retinal image rendered from the vantage point of the fish's cyclopean vision sensor. Fig. 6.4 and 6.5 shows examples of retinal images acquired by a fish "witnessing" another fish falling prey to a fishing line.

**Figures 6.4.** Fisheye view of the world showing fishing line. See the original color image in Appendix D

**Figures 6.5.** Fisheye view of the world showing hooked fish

## 6.4 Computing Visibility

An object is "visible" if any part of it enters the view volume and is not fully occluded by another object. To determine visibility, we associate with the vision sensor the fish's local right-handed coordinate system $(X_f, Y_f, Z_f)$ (see Fig. 6.6 or Fig. 4.12). The $x$-axis is along the fish's spinal axis and the $y$-axis points to the fish's left.

### 6.4.1 Visibility of a Point

To determine if some point $P$ is visible, we shoot a ray from the cyclopean origin $O$ (on $X_f$ and near the fish's mouth) to $P$ (see Fig. 6.6). First, if $\|P - O\| \leq V_r$ and the angle between the ray and the fish's $x$-axis is less than 150 degrees then $P$ is within the view volume. Second, to examine if $P$ is occluded, we test if the ray intersects other objects (fishes or static obstacles) in the fish's view volume.

**Occlusion Test.** Fishes are generally vigorous animals that move around constantly. If at some instant the sight of one fish is blocked by another fish passing by, the occlusion will most likely be cleared soon after – since both fish are in motion. The temporary blocking of sight should not result in abrupt changes in a fish's behavior. Therefore, occlusion tests against another fish tend to be unessential. To increase computational efficiency, the artificial fish performs occlusion tests only against large static environmental objects. In

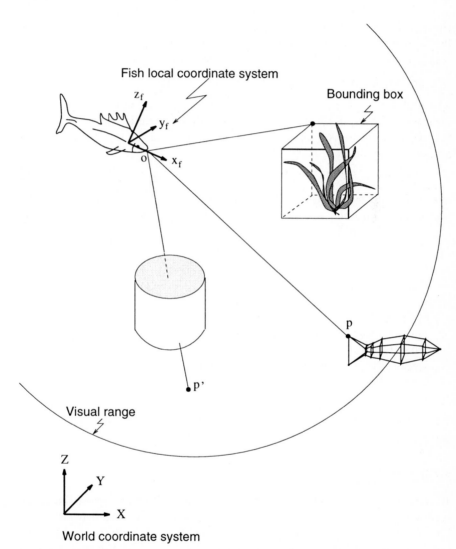

Fish local coordinate system

Bounding box

$z_f$

$y_f$

$o$    $x_f$

p

p'

Visual range

Z

Y

X

World coordinate system

**Figures 6.6.** Occlusion test: point $P$ is visible while point $P'$ is occluded

the current implementation, this includes cylindrical objects. Note that, for obstacles with more complex geometric shapes, cylinders can serve as their bounding boxes.

The algorithm for testing the intersection of a ray with a cylinder is simple, especially since the axis of each cylinder is parallel to the $z$-axis of the world coordinate system (see Fig. 6.6). Let the coordinates of $O$ and $P$ in the world coordinate system be denoted by $(x_o, y_o, z_o)$ and $(x_p, y_p, z_p)$, respectively. Then line $\overline{OP}$ can be represented by the parametric equation

$$x = x_o + t\Delta x, \quad y = y_o + t\Delta y, \quad z = z_o + t\Delta z, \tag{6.1}$$

where $\Delta x = x_p - x_o$, $\Delta y = y_p - y_o$, $\Delta z = z_p - z_o$ and $t \in [0, 1]$. Let $r$ denote the radius and $h$ the height of the cylinder $C$ under consideration. Its projection onto the $XY$-plane is a circle $A$ which can be represented by the parametric equation

$$(x - a)^2 + (y - b)^2 = r^2 \tag{6.2}$$

where $(a, b, 0)$ denotes the center of $A$. The occlusion-test algorithm we develop can be outlined as follows (all calculations are performed in the world coordinate system):

1. *Check if line $\overline{OP}$ intersects with circle $A$:*
   Substitute the $x$ and $y$ in Eq. (6.2) with those in Eq. (6.1) and solve for $t$. If the solutions $t_1$ and $t_2$ ($t_1 \leq t_2$) have real values and at least one of them is in $[0, 1]$, then do step 2; Otherwise, stop ($P$ is not occluded by cylinder $C$).
2. *Further check if line $\overline{OP}$ intersects with cylinder $C$:*
   Substitute the $t$ in Eq. (6.1) with $t_1$ and $t_2$ to get the points of intersection. In fact, one only needs to calculate $z_i = z_o + t_i\Delta z$, $i = 1, 2$. If $0 < z_i \leq h$ for $i = 1$ or $i = 2$, then point $P$ is occluded. Otherwise, $P$ is visible.

This algorithm is essentially an 'extent testing' algorithm commonly used in determining visibility of objects in a scene [109].

### 6.4.2 Visibility of Another Fish

To determine the visibility of another fish, we take advantage of the mass-spring-damper structure of the fish model. To first determine if fish $j$ is within fish $i$'s view volume, we simply test if the center of $j$'s body $Q_j$ (we use the origin of the fish local coordinate system $(X_f, Y_f, Z_f)$ as the center point) falls within the view volume of $i$ (Note that, the view volume of fish $i$ is $s_j^p V_r$ instead of $V_r$). If it is, we proceed as follows: Fish $j$ is visible to fish $i$ if and only if any one of the mass points of $j$ is visible to $i$ (i.e. not occluded by any other objects). In Fig. 6.6, the fish represented by the mass-spring-damper model is visible. It should be pointed out that, although in the worst case this visibility check can be expensive (each fish has 23 nodes), on average it is much better since the algorithm will reach a conclusion as soon as it finds a single visible node. In the case of a more complicated virtual environment, we can use bounding box techniques to speed up the occlusion test.

### 6.4.3 Visibility of a Cylinder

Since a full visibility check for a cylinder would be computationally expensive, we perform the following simple test: Let $P$ be the point on the axis of cylinder $C$ that is closest in height to the cyclopean origin $O$. Then we say that $C$ is visible if $||P - O|| - r < V_r$, where $r$ is the radius of $C$. Since the cylinders in a typical virtual marine world in our animation are fairly scattered, the occlusion test is neglected.

### 6.4.4 Visibility of Seaweeds

In our animated marine world, we model clustered seaweeds (multiple leaves originated from the same root) that are often observed in nature. To perform efficient visibility check of seaweeds, we use a rectangular bounding box for each seaweed cluster (see Fig. 6.6). The visibility of a seaweed cluster is determined by the visibility of the 8 corners of the corresponding bounding box. If any of the corner points is visible, the seaweed cluster is visible.

### 6.4.5 Discussion

To summarize, in order to model an artificial fish's perceptual capability, at each animation time step, a visibility check with all environmental objects is performed. As we described above, the visibility check consists of two steps: First, the *view volume test* checks if an object is in the fish's view volume and, if it is, the *occlusion test* checks whether it is occluded.

Since the occlusion test algorithm is only performed against, hopefully, a small number of objects that fall within the fish's view volume, the corresponding computational cost does not increase linearly with the total number of objects in the scene. However, this is not true for the computation in the view volume test: If a naive algorithm is used, the computational cost involved (for each fish) is $O(N)$ where $N$ is the number of objects in the scene. The total cost for all the fish performing the view volume test will increase quadratically with the number of fish in the animation. Therefore, when the number of fish is large, for example, when animating a school of fish, a more efficient algorithm for the view volume test is desirable. To this end, we have implemented an algorithm that exploits the space-time coherence of objects. We associate, with each fish, a list of *potentially-visible objects*. One can view the potentially-visible objects as those that fall within a pseudo view volume that has a larger radius than that of the fish's view volume. This list is generated at the beginning of the animation and is only updated intermittently. At each animation time step, assuming constraints on the maximum velocity of the fishes, instead of performing the view volume test on all the other objects, a fish need only check if any of the objects in the list of potentially-visible objects enters the view volume.

It is important to appreciate, however, that the value of our perception model does not lie in the particular method we choose to implement it. (Indeed, to achieve high simulation speed for animation, we have chosen a very simple approach which may not be readily extensible to a more complex virtual environment.) Rather our main purpose is to demonstrate the importance of simulating perceptual capability to the modeling of realistic behavior and, in this respect, our approach is adequate for the task at hand.

One avenue for future research would be to implement a more sophisticated geometric method that can scale well to more complicated virtual environments. For instance, we could tessellate the entire 3D environment into, say, $M$ cells and establish a look-up table with $M$ entries. Each entry of the table registers the indices of objects that reside in the corresponding cell. This table is computed at the beginning of the animation and is updated for each fish at each time step. Because of space-time coherence, the update need not be computed with respect to all the cells. Rather only the adjacent cells are checked to see in which new cell a fish is currently situated. Once the table is updated, the objects that fall within a fish's view volume can be easily determined by accessing the table entries of those cells that are nearby. This algorithm is especially suitable if there is a large number of objects besides fish, such as static obstacles, seaweeds, etc.

Moreover, for the occlusion test, more sophisticated bounding volume algorithms, such as the Kay-Kajiya algorithm [109], can be employed when the shape of the obstacles is more complicated.

## 6.5 The Focusser

The task of a focus of attention mechanism is to extract the appropriate aspects of the world for the particular tasks with which the animal/agent is concerned. Robotics and computer vision researchers have proposed a number of computational models of attention mechanisms for various applications [110]. Modeling focus of attention in artificial animals is important for modeling their behavior as well as for gaining higher computational efficiency in sensory processing.

### 6.5.1 Focus of Attention in Animals

Animals are believed to focus their attention in two ways. The first, which is most common in lower animals, is the use of specialized sensing organs. Many of these animals have severely limited, but highly specialized vision which allow them to see just what they *need* to see in order to function successfully in their environments [108]. For example, anteater's eyes are placed very low in their heads and they have only monocular vision but with extremely high acuity. Birds, on the other hand, have excellent binocular vision that is good for judging distances. The second way can be thought of as cognitive, where the animals only perceive what they attend to; i.e., they pay attention only to what is important in their particular situation at hand.

> *Under certain circumstances nesting herring-gulls behave as though their eggs were invisible to them. If, in the gull's absence, the eggs are removed and put just outside the nest the parent bird will retrieve them, but if the distance is made a little greater the bird will sit happily on the empty nest with the eggs in full sight. That the eggs can be seen perfectly well is indicated by removing them still further away, the gull will then eat them as it does its neighbour's eggs if it should find them unguarded. Herring-gull chicks show camouflage colouring very similar to that of the eggs but the parent bird never has any difficulty in seeing and recognizing its own chicks. There is nothing wrong with the herring-gull's eyes. The explanation of the different reactions to eggs and chicks appears to be that, under normal circumstances, the eggs do not leave the nest and it is, therefore, sufficient if the parent knows the position of the nest, while the active chicks often wander away and have to be got back [108].*

The best example of a natural attention mechanism that employs both mechanical and cognitive means may lie in the vision of humans and animals. The retinal image from an eye has in its center a high-acuity region known as the *fovea*, beyond which the image resolution drops in the visual *periphery*. Humans and animals, motivated by their behavioral needs, are able to focus their sight (by moving their eyes or turning their heads) onto the object of interest such that an accurate image of that object is obtained in their foveas while its immediate surroundings fall into the low-resolution peripheral region.

### 6.5.2 Design of the Focusser

The design of the focusser is inspired by the functioning of the eyes. It synthesizes the foveal vision by suppressing sensory information unrelated to object(s) of interest. It also synthesizes peripheral vision by generating qualitative *motor preferences* from related environmental conditions. As we shall see, the motor preferences are important to the artificial animal's behavior.

**Obtaining the Focus.** As we shall describe in the next chapter, an intention generator in the artificial fish's brain generates an intention of what to do next at each animation time step. The functioning of the focusser is controlled by the time-varying intention of the fish. When the intention is to *avoid* collision, the focusser is activated to locate the position of the most dangerous obstacle, usually the closest, among all the dangerous obstacles perceived (we will explain the determination of dangerous obstacles in the next section). The focusser passes only the position of the most dangerous obstacle to the behavior system. Likewise, when the intention of a male fish is to *mate*, the focusser targets the most desirable female fish; when the intention is to *escape* from predators, only the detailed information about the most threatening predator gets passed through the focusser.

**Motor Preferences.** The above simple attention mechanism passes only the directly required information for fulfilling the animal's current intention. While this is highly efficient, it neglects some desirable sensory information necessary for better accomplishing the task at hand, or for taking compromised actions towards satisfying more than one intention. An important characteristic of animal behavior is to be able to select compromised actions from the consideration of multiple aspects of the animal's behavior and its environment [91]. In order to capture this feature in an artificial animal's behavior model, sensory information in addition to that provided about the object of focus is required.

*Example 1:*

Take for example the case where a fish intends to avoid collisions with surrounding obstacles, among which one presents the highest danger of collision. In most situations, the fish would have several choices of actions that it can take to maneuver around that obstacle: it can turn left, turn right, retreat, etc. Further assume that there is another nearby obstacle (either mobile or static) which is to the left of the fish and a food source to the right. With the focusser described above, sensory information about this other obstacle and the food source will be filtered out and hence cannot contribute to the decision about the choice of action. However, by considering the presence of this additional sensory information, the obvious choice of action would be to take a right turn. If the fish retreats, it cannot take advantage of eating food. If it takes a left turn the obstacle to the left would immediately become the next "most dangerous" obstacle and hence, in the worst case, the fish would dither back and forth.

*Example 2:*

Another example is concerned with attempting to satisfy multiple desires. Imagine that a hungry fish is chasing floating food particles. Assume the simple case of two food particles, one located straight ahead and closer to the fish, and the other a little further and to the left of the fish. Under normal conditions, the fish will focus its attention on the food that requires the least amount of effort to get – the particle in front of it. However, suppose the fish has also a desire to mate and it sees a potential mate to its left, then a better choice (a compromised choice) of action may be to turn left – such that it can eat food while approaching the potential mate. This also depends on the relative strength of the desire to mate compared to the intention to eat.

It is clear that additional information about the environment is necessary for selecting preferred strategies of action. But how accurate and complete should additional information about the environmental objects be?

At one end of the spectrum we could use a complete, accurate description (i.e., 3D positions, velocities, etc., of all relevant objects), it is possible to decide on an 'optimal' action at a given moment, such as "turn right 23.65 degrees". However, this will involve high computational cost and hence off-set the benefits of focus of attention. In addition, the artificial fish's motor system, like those of many real animals, cannot produce motions more accurate than, say, turn roughly 45 degrees. Therefore excessively accurate motor commands tend to be futile. At the other end of the spectrum we could have no additional information whatsoever, but as we have already stated, this is undesirable. So the question remains: What level of granularity should our system have in between the two extremes? Inspired by the fact that the peripheral vision of the human eye, although of poor accuracy, serves the necessary purpose. We chose to represent the additional information as qualitative recommendations of actions, henceforth referred to as *motor preferences.*

Instead of passing all the sensory information about the surroundings, the focusser computes and collects a set of motor preferences. The set of motor preferences corresponds to the set of motor skills of the artificial fish, namely, M(LEFT), M(RIGHT), M(FORWARD), M(BACKWARD), M(ASCEND), M(DESCEND).

First let us distinguish the concept of 'intention' from that of 'desire'. Desires are potential candidates of the intention. At any given moment, an agent can have multiple desires, but there will be only one intention which corresponds to the strongest desire. Now if a sensory stimulus relevant to a desire/intention occurs, a value is assigned to the appropriate motor preference. A positive value represents a positive recommendation for the action, and a negative value represents negative recommendation for the action. For instance, if an obstacle is close and is in front of the fish, a negative value will be assigned to M(FORWARD). The magnitude of the value is given by a factor $\tau \in [0,1]$ representing the strength of that desire. The final value of a motor preference will be a normalized sum of all the assigned values from different desires. The summation is performed first on all the positive recommendations and then on all negative recommendations. These two summations are individually normalized and then added together. For example, suppose a fish perceives three potential mates to its left and the desire to mate has strength $\tau^m$ (we will describe how the $\tau$'s are calculated in Section 7.6 in Chapter 7). Now further suppose that the fish also detects a predator to its left and the desire to flee has strength $\tau^f$. Then the motor preference $M(\text{LEFT}) = (3\tau^m/3) - \tau^f = \tau^m - \tau^f$. Therefore, in the first example described above, there are two motor preferences: $M(\text{LEFT}) = -\tau^a$ ($^a$ represents the desire to avoid collision) and $M(\text{RIGHT}) = \tau^e$ ($^e$ represents the desire to eat).

### 6.5.3 Summary

To summarize, the focusser delivers to the appropriate behavior component the accurate sensory information about the object of interest as well as the motor preferences reflecting the current environmental conditions. This design not only provides highly focussed attention for efficiency, but also allows influence from environmental conditions to achieve compromised actions.

As is indicated by the examples in the previous section, motor preferences are used in two ways. In the first way they are used to influence the choice of a proper action. This is done by influencing both the selection of a proper motor skill (e.g., example 1 above) and the calculation of the corresponding control parameters. In the case where all possible actions are accompanied by equal-strength negative motor preferences, an action gets chosen at random and the corresponding control parameters (angle or speed) are modified to accommodate the preference. For example, suppose the `right-turn-MC` is chosen and the calculated angle of turn is $\beta$, since $M(RIGHT) = -\tau$, the final, compromised angle of turn will be $\min[1.0, (1.5 - \tau)]\beta$. Similar modification of motor control parameters is also performed in the case where the chosen action is accompanied by a negative preference. Positive preferences do not have any effect on the control parameters.

In the second way, the motor preferences are used to help the focusser locate the object of interest. This process demonstrates a certain level of compromise among different desires. Typical cases include targeting the most desirable food source and mating partner. In each case, there is an evaluation criterion according to which a real valued 'desirability' $D_i \in [0, 1]$ is calculated for each potential target $i$ (i.e. food source or mate). Assuming $1 \leq i \leq n$ where $n$ is the number of potential targets, then the procedure for choosing the most desirable target can be specified in pseudo code (D[i] represents $D_i$):

```
for (i = 1:n)
   sort(D[i]); // D[1] has the largest value.
if (n==1 || D[1]>>D[2])
   target := 1;
else {
   K := min[N, n]; // N is a small integer. Typically, N=3.
   for (k = 1:K) {
      calculate RelPos[k]; // RelPos[k] is the relative position
   // of (k) to fish and its possible
                           // values are: left, right, front
      p := 0.2;           // is a small weight factor
      D[k] += p*M(RelPos[k]); // M(front) = M(FORWARD)
   }
   for (k = 1:K)
      D[i] := max{D[k]};
   target := i;
}
```

The desirability calculation for a food source is, for simplicity, solely based on its distance to the fish. Let $d_i$ be the distance of food $i$ to the fish, then

$D_i = 1.0 - d_i/O_r$ where $O_r$ is the fish's perceptual range described earlier. The desirability of a mating partner will be described in Section 7.9.3.

## 6.6 From Perception to Behavior

The perception system supports a range of fish behaviors, such as foraging and escaping from predation. This section describes how perception supports behavior through the example of collision avoidance – the most basic perception-driven behavior in the artificial fish's behavior repertoire.

### 6.6.1 An Example: Collision Detection

Collision avoidance is essential for the day to day life of animals. Their survival needs compel them to move around constantly. To be able to do so safely, an animal's perception must first provide an account for collision detection.

Analogous to all animals and humans, the avoidance of collisions with obstacles is a primitive behavior that an artificial fish performs. Once a static obstacle or another fish comes into view, the artificial fish must determine if there is potential for a collision and, if so, act to avoid the collision. As will be shown in Chapter 7, the collision detection algorithms described below support the realistic modeling of collision avoidance and hence is essential for the realistic modeling of the artificial fish's behavior on the whole.

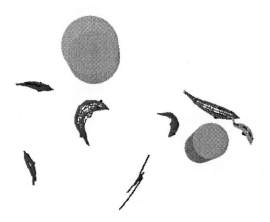

**Figures 6.7.** Swimming fishes avoiding collisions with cylindrical obstacles

**Detecting Danger of Collision with Cylindrical Obstacles.** Fig. 6.7 shows several swimming fishes avoiding collisions with cylindrical obstacles. The collision test against a visible cylinder $C$ is performed using similar algorithms to those used for the occlusion test. We define a ray along the fish's local $x$-axis $X_f$ which starts at the cyclopean origin $O$ and ends at point $Q$. One can imagine ray $\overline{OQ}$ as an "antenna" of the fish that detects potential danger of collision. The length of $\overline{OQ}$ defines the range of detection (in our implementation, we set this length to be the fish's body length). Taking into account the fish's body width $f_w$, we perform the collision test against radius $r + 1.5f_w$ instead of $r$ ($r$ is the radius of $C$). The pseudo code for this test is as follows ($z_1$, $z_2$ and $h$ are defined as in the occlusion test algorithm):

```
if (OQ intersects with the boundary of C) {
                        // there may be a threat of collision
    fh := body height of fish;
    if (min[z1, z2] < h + fh)  // check if fish is well above C
      return(threat of collision);
    else
      return(no threat of collision);
} else
    return(no threat of collision);
```

If threat of collision is detected from more than one static obstacles, the one whose boundary is closest to the fish's cyclopean origin is regarded as the most dangerous obstacle.

**Detecting Danger of Collision with Other Fish.** To determine if there is a threat of collision with a visible fish we introduce a *collision sensitivity region*. It works in a similar manner as the antenna ray $\overline{OQ}$ used above. A collision sensitivity region is a region of $\Re^3$ wherein any object intersecting with it is considered to present a collision threat. The different sizes of the sensitivity region associated with different fishes can result in different 'disposition': a large sensitivity region results in a 'timid' fish that takes evasive action to avoid a potential collision well in advance, while a tight sensitivity region yields a 'courageous' fish that takes evasive action at the last second.

Let the *center line* of a fish be the line through the mean positions of the following sets of nodes: $\{0\}, \{1, 2, 3, 4\}, \ldots, \{17, 18, 19, 20\}, \{21, 22\}$ (see Fig. 4.2; larger fishes need a finer sampling and this is done by interpolating the center line). For efficiency we choose to represent the collision sensitivity region as a rectangular box, see Fig. 6.8. Fish $i$ presents a threat of collision to fish $k$ if any node on $i$'s center line falls within $k$'s collision sensitivity region. The size of a fish's collision sensitivity region may be varied according to behavioral needs, as will be seen in the next chapter. If more than one other fish present a collision threat, the one with the largest portion of its center line in fish $i$'s sensitivity region is regarded as being the most dangerous.

## Sensitivity Region

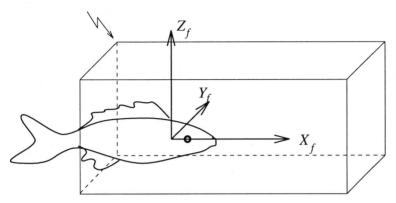

**Figures 6.8.** The fish's collision sensitivity region

## 6.7 Synthetic Vision Models

As we have mentioned earlier, when the virtual environment becomes highly complex, for example, when the shapes of the obstacles or other objects are highly irregular, more sophisticated geometric methods for perception modeling can be employed. An alternative approach to geometric methods is one that involves building synthetic vision models of animals.

In the context of artificial life, we may also be interested in developing models of animal vision that are biologically more faithful. For instance, we may be interested in modeling the process of extracting useful perceptual information from the retinal images of an animal's vision system and studying how this process affects an animal's behavior.

Synthetic vision models can be built based on the animated retinal images rendered from an artificial animal's "point of view". One obvious advantage of this approach is that the retinal images readily respect the occlusion relationships between objects in the animal's view. In addition, these retinal images are perspective projections of the 3D virtual world and hence are biologically plausible models of animal vision. Some aspects of animal perception, such as the recognition of object textures or environmental illumination, cannot be captured by geometric methods but are unique properties that have to be extracted from images. The synthetic vision approach for animation was first explored by Renault, Magnenat-Thalmann, and Thalmann [69] in guiding synthetic actors' navigation through a dynamic world.

A simple procedure of synthetic vision is to render each object in the scene with a unique shaded color (i.e. color coding the objects). That way, by examining the presence of different colored pixels in the image, we know which objects can be seen (in the visual field and not occluded). The range of an object may be either obtained directly from the graphics database or computed by using its relative positions in the binocular images. Since the images are rendered with perspective projection, a collision test against an object may be performed by taking into account the relative size of that object in the images. Object identification can be made more efficient by using similar shaded colors for objects in the same category. For example, we can render all fishes with different shades of red, and all cylindrical obstacles with different shades of blue, etc., such that a quick pre-processing of the image can reveal the presence of certain kinds of objects. Such identity maps and range maps can be thought of as the analogues of *intrinsic images* [111] of the scene. Fig. 6.9a(a) shows an example of the binocular retinal images, Fig. 6.9a(b) shows the corresponding color-coded identity maps, and Fig. 6.9a(c) shows the range maps generated by assigning each pixel a color of gray according to its z-value. The further an object is, the darker is its color.

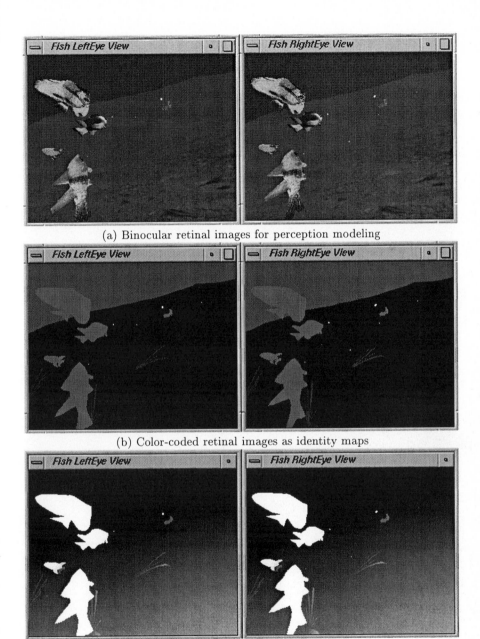

(a) Binocular retinal images for perception modeling

(b) Color-coded retinal images as identity maps

(c) Binocular range maps

**Figures 6.9a.** Analogues of intrinsic images

# 7. The Behavior System

Action selection in the artificial fish is controlled by its behavior system. The behavior system consists of the habits and mental state of the fish, an intention generator and a set of behavior routines (Fig. 7.1). The behavior system runs continuously within the fish's simulation loop. At each time step the intention generator issues an intention based on the fish's habits, mental state, and incoming sensory information. It then chooses and executes a behavior routine which in turn selects and runs the appropriate motor controllers. It is important to note that the behavior routines are incremental by design. Their job is to get the artificial fish one step closer to fulfilling its intention during the current time step. Moreover, at any given moment in time, there is only one intention or one active behavior in the artificial fish's behavior system. This hypothesis is commonly made by ethologists when analyzing the behavior of fishes, birds and four-legged animals of or below intermediate complexity (e.g. dogs, cats) [93, 16].

In this chapter, we first list a set of design criteria for effective action selection mechanisms that guides our design of the behavior system. Next we discuss the implementation scheme we choose for the behavior control (or action selection) of the artificial fish, considering especially the overall structure of the different control levels and stages. We then describe in more detail how this is implemented via the intention generator and the behavior routines. In addition, we explain how some of the primitive behaviors, such as collision avoidance and moving target pursuit, as well as some of the more complex, motivational behaviors, such as schooling and mating, are generated. We also introduce the different types of artificial fishes that we have implemented to date. Finally, we present results and discuss possible improvements to our design.

## 7.1 Effective Action Selection Mechanisms

Motivated by theories from ethology, artificial life researchers have proposed a set of design criteria for effective action selection mechanisms [80, 81, 77]. The following criteria are the basis of the behavior modeling in the artificial fish:

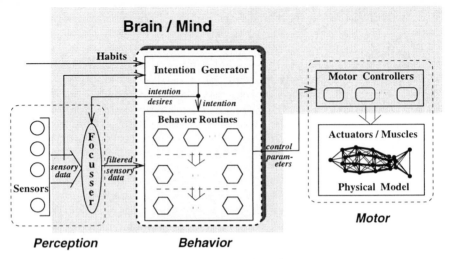

**Figures 7.1.** The behavior system in an artificial fish

1. Priority of behaviors. For example, avoiding life-threatening situations should take precedence over other behaviors.
2. Persistence (or hysteresis) in behavior so that animals do not dither.
3. Compromised actions.
4. Opportunism. This refers to the temporary interruption of the ongoing behavior and the subsequent launching of another behavior which, potentially, can benefit the animal within a short period of time or with little effort. For example, if a nesting herring-gull sees food on its way to fetch stones for its nest, it may detour and eat before resuming nest building behavior.
5. Quick response time.

## 7.2 Behavior Control and Ethology

> It is often possible to break down complex behavior patterns into smaller units, some of which are immediately equitable with reflexes. Behavior is frequently organized in a hierarchical way ... Thus the higher control systems must compete for control of reflexes rather in the manner that reflexes compete for control of muscles.
> – A. Manning

The behavior control scheme in our artificial animal can be viewed as consisting of two important relationships. One relationship is between the motor controllers and muscles/fins, and the other is between some higher control mechanisms and the motor controllers. The motor controllers coordinate and control the muscles and fins in order to form useful motor skills while, in a similar manner, higher control mechanisms compete for the control of the motor controllers to generate meaningful behaviors. This paradigm is consistent with the animal behavior theory proposed by the ethologist Manning [16].

In our framework, the higher control mechanisms correspond to the fish's behavior system, where the action selection process – the competition over the control of the motor controllers – happens at two levels: the *intention* level and the *action* level. Intentions are governed by the intention generator and actions are governed by the focusser and the behavior routines. Fig. 7.2 illustrates the overall control scheme for action selection in the artificial fish.

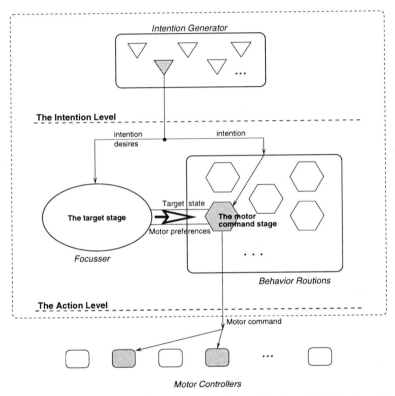

**Figures 7.2.** The control scheme for action selection. Shaded elements represent the currently active elements. Note that non-exclusive motor skills can be selected simultaneously

## 7.2.1 The Intention Level

At the intention level, different desires compete over *what* should be done (which desire is to become the current intention), given the animal's external and internal conditions. This process can be well explained by a typical scene generated in our simulation: A fish is heading towards food when it encounters an obstacle in the way. It makes appropriate turns in order to avoid colliding with the obstacle, and once the obstacle is cleared it resumes pursuing the food. Such a behavioral sequence is the result of the competition between the desire to eat food and the desire to avoid collision.

## 7.2.2 The Action Level

Even when an intention has been decided, it remains to determine *how* the intention should be fulfilled through the successive selection of motor actions. The selected sequence of actions, hence the behavioral outcome, depends on the dynamics of the 3D virtual world as well as the dynamics of the multiple desires of the fish. The latter manifests its effect through the motor preferences and hence, although there is only one intention or winning behavior at any instant in time, other behaviors can nonetheless influence the creature's actions.

We can further analyze the control at this level at two stages – the *target* stage where the target, i.e. the object of interest given the current intention, is chosen and the *motor command* stage where the final, detailed motor command is calculated. The target stage control is governed by the focusser and the motor command stage control is governed by the behavior routines.

The control process at the target stage can be viewed as the 'competition' amongst the set of potential targets to become the current target. This is particularly obvious in the cases described in Section 6.5.3, where the fish tries to decide to which food morsel or mate it should attend. Since the desirability of each potential target may change over time (due to the dynamics of the virtual world and the motor preferences), the target may change over time. Consider the case when the fish intends to eat and there are multiple available food sources; it is possible that a fish may perform an interesting zigzagging behavior due to the competition between potential targets.

Once the current target is chosen, control is then passed to the active behavior routine. The final choice of a motor controller and the appropriate control parameters are computed based on the current state of the fish and the target, as well as the values of the motor preferences (see Section 6.5.3 for examples and details).

## 7.2.3 Summary

The intricacy of the behaviors we have been able to emulate in the artificial fishes results from the dynamic interactions between different intentions and between different choices of actions. The separation of the intention level and the action level in the behavioral control and action selection scheme makes the design more intuitive and efficient. In particular, since the function of the intention generator is independent from those of the behavior routines, new behaviors can be added into the behavior repertoire in steps: First, the behavior routine of a new behavior can be written and tested independently from the intention generator (and from other behavior routines that are not a component routine). The intention generator can then be modified to incorporate the new intention and can also be tested independently.

In the following sections, we describe the implementation of the intention generator, the behavior routines, and how they work in conjunction with the perception system to govern effective action selection in an artificial fish. We start with the fish's static habits and its dynamic mental state.

## 7.3 Habits

The animator establishes the innate characteristic of each artificial fish through a set of binary habit parameters. These parameters determine whether the fish is male or female, and whether it likes, dislikes, or does not care about

1. brightness,
2. darkness,
3. cold,
4. warmth,
5. schooling.

'Does not care' is represented by assigning identical values to the two contradicting habit parameters. For instance, if both brightness and darkness parameters are assigned '1' or '0' then the fish does not care about the lighting patterns in its environment.

## 7.4 Mental State

Unlike a fish's habits, which are static, its mental state varies over time. The mental state of an animal can be viewed as consisting of several distinct desires. For example, the desire to drink or the desire to eat. In order to model an artificial fish's mental state, it is important to make certain that the modeled desires resemble the three fundamental properties of natural desires: (a) they should be time varying; (b) they should depend on either internal urge or external stimuli or both; (c) they should be satisfiable (see Section 7.4 for more details).

Currently, the artificial fish has three mental state variables, hunger $H$, libido $L$, and fear $F$. The range of each variable is $[0, 1]$, with higher values indicating a stronger desire to eat, mate and avoid predators, respectively. $H$ and $L$ are determined both by internal urge and by external sensory stimuli, while $F$ is solely induced by the latter, i.e., the perception of predators. The variables are calculated as follows (overlined terms simulate the corresponding internal urge):

$$H(t) = \min\left[\overline{1 - n^e(t)r(\Delta t^H)/n^a} + \alpha_h S^h(t),\ 1\right],$$

$$L(t) = \min\left[\overline{l(\Delta t^L)(1 - H(t))} + \alpha_l S^l(t),\ 1\right],$$

$$F(t) = \min\left[\sum_i F^i,\ 1\right], \text{ where } F^i = \min[D_0/d^i(t), 1],$$

where

$t$ is time,

$n^e(t)$ is the amount of food consumed as measured by the number of food particles or prey fishes eaten,

$r(x) = 1 - p_0 x$ with constant $p_0$ is the digestion rate,

$\Delta t^H$ is the time since the last meal,

$n^a$ is a constant that indicates the appetite of the fish (bigger fishes have a larger $n^a$),

$\alpha_h S^h(t)$ captures the influence of external sensory stimuli, i.e. the perception of nearby food (explained in more detail shortly),

$l(x) = p_1 x$ with constant $p_1$ is the libido function,

$\Delta t^L$ is the time since the last mating,

$\alpha_l S^l(t)$ calculates the influence of the perception of potential mates;

$D_0 = 200$ is a constant,

$F^i$ and $d^i$ are, respectively, the fear of and distance to sighted predator $i$.

Nominal constants are $p_0 = 0.00067$ and $p_1 = 0.0025$. Certain choices can result in ravenous fishes (e.g, $p_0 = 0.005$) or sexual mania (e.g., $p_1 = 0.01$) or cowards (e.g., $D_0 = 500$).

**Opportunism.** The significance of simulating explicitly the influence of external stimuli on $H$ and $L$ is that it gives rise to opportunism. Opportunism is an important aspect of animal behavior and has been especially addressed by researchers in designing action selection mechanisms for animats [88, 81, 90]. We model opportunism to increase the realism of the behavior of the artificial fishes.

It is reasonable to assume that the mental state of hunger and libido are governed mainly by the corresponding internal urge, while external stimuli will have an impact only if they are strong enough. This indicates that $S^h(t)$ and $S^l(t)$ should resemble a step function. The detailed calculations are as follows. For efficiency, we assume that only the stimulus of the *closest* food and mate contributes to $S^h(t)$ and $S^l(t)$, respectively. In addition, the strength of such a stimulus depends solely on the time-varying distance $d(t)$ between the stimulant and the fish – the smaller the $d(t)$, the stronger the stimulus. Let $s(t) = 1/d(t)$ denote the strength of the stimuli, then $S^h(t)$ and $S^l(t)$ are given by

$$S^x(t) = \begin{cases} 0 & \text{if } s(t) \le q_1 \\ \frac{s(t)-q_1}{2q_2-q_1-s(t)} & \text{if } q_1 \le s(t) \le q_2 \\ 1.0 & \text{otherwise} \end{cases} ,$$

where $x$ denotes either $h$ or $l$ and $q_1$, $q_2$ are threshold values. When $x = $'$h$', we use $q_1 = 0.05$ and $q_2 = 0.2$; When $x = $'$l$', we use $q_1 = 0.025$ and $q_2 = 0.1$. A graph of $S^h(t)$ and $S^l(t)$ is shown in Fig. 7.3. The parameters are $\alpha_h = 0.8$ and $\alpha_l = 0.5$ in our implementation.

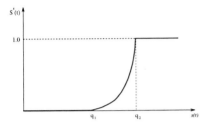

**Figures 7.3.** The form of the stimulus functions $S^h(t)$ and $S^l(t)$

**Satiation of a Desire.** An important principle of animal behavior, as pointed out by many ethologists [17, 112, 16], is the feedback from the result of the animal's earlier actions. This feature is well reflected in our models of the mental state variables and corresponds to the "satisfiability" of the desires. As will be shown in the next section, the mental state variables are directly responsible for activating the matching behaviors. If a behavior is successful, its outcome should be able to satisfy, albeit perhaps gradually, the desire that triggered the behavior in the first place. It is essential to model satisfiability, otherwise a behavior may never terminate once activated.

The formulation of the mental state variables exhibits satisfiability as follows: The value of $F$ depends only on the strength of the external stimulus. This means that if the appropriate stimulus does not exist or is weak, $F$ will remain low (or satiated). This can be achieved by two means – first, the reactive fleeing action of the fish and, second, the dynamic nature of the virtual world. The values of $H$ and $L$ are mainly controlled by the corresponding internal urge component whose value decreases as the result of successful feeding and mating. The external stimulus components, as we have shown, represent dynamic opportunities and hence are kept at low values under normal conditions.

Note that in the formulation of $H$, the internal urge component restrains the stimulus component such that the fish will not keep taking opportunities to eat food (even when opportunities keep presenting themselves) to the exclusion of all other behaviors. For example, once the amount of food taken $n^e$ exceeds twice the value of the fish's appetite $n^a$, then $H$ becomes zero. This situation continues until $r(\Delta t^H) \le 0$ indicating the complete digestion of the food, at which moment, $n^e$ is reset to zero.

## 7.5 Intention Generator

Fig. 7.4 illustrates a simplified generic intention generator which is responsible for the goal-directed behavior of the artificial fish in its dynamic world.

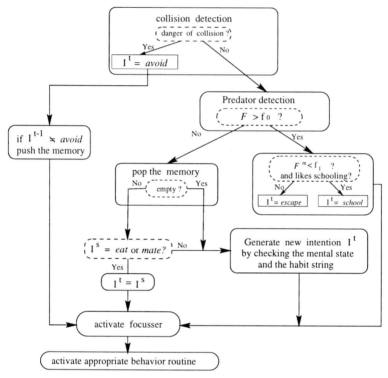

**Figures 7.4.** Generic intention generator (simplified). Set of intentions: { *avoid, escape, school, eat, mate, leave, wander* }. $f_0$ and $f_1$ are thresholds with $f_0 < f_1$

The intention generator is based on a priority hierarchy of behaviors. Life threatening behaviors, such as collision avoidance, have highest priority. As indicated in the figure, the intention generator first checks the sensory information stream to see if there is any immediate danger of collision. If there is (see Chapter 6 for collision test) then the intention $I$ generated is to *avoid* collision. If there is no immediate danger of collision, the neighborhood is searched for predators, the fear state variable $F$ and the most dangerous predator $m$ for which $F^m \geq F^i$ (for any predator $i$) are calculated. If the total fear $F > f_0$ (where $0.1 \leq f_0 \leq 0.5$ is a threshold value) evasive action is to be taken. If the most dangerous predator is not too threatening (i.e. $F^m < f_1$ where $f_1 > f_0$) and the fish has a schooling habit, then the *school* intention is generated, otherwise the *escape* intention is generated.

If fear is below threshold and the behavior memory (more details are in Section 7.7 below) is empty, the hunger and libido mental state variables $H$ and $L$ are calculated. If the greater of the two exceeds a threshold $0 < r < 0.5$, the intention generated will be to *eat* or *mate* accordingly. If $H = L > r$, then $I^{t-1}$ is checked to see if it is one of the two intentions *eat* and *mate*. If not, one of them gets chosen at random, otherwise $I^t = I^{t-1}$.

If the above test fails, the intention generator accesses the ambient light and temperature information from the perception system. If the fish's habits imply contentment with the ambient conditions, the intention generated will be to *wander* about, otherwise it will be to *leave* the vicinity. Note that, unlike the desire to eat, to mate or to escape which are modeled explicitly by the mental state variables, the desire to avoid collision, to school, to wander and to leave are modeled implicitly by their intrinsic behavioral priorities (level in the hierarchy), sensory stimuli and innate habits. The following diagram shows all the desires ordered according to their levels in the priority hierarchy:

Desire to avoid collision

⇓

Desire to flee from predator

⇓

Desire to eat,     Desire to mate

⇓

Desire to school

⇓

Desire to wander,     Desire to leave

### 7.5.1 Why Hierarchy?

**Ethological Background.** Ethologists have long believed that the control of action selection in animals is hierarchical in structure [72, 93, 113]. This classical view is supported by extensive observation of and numerous experiments on animal behavior. Tinbergen [93] described a "working hypothesis" of an action selection mechanism composed of a hierarchy of nodes. The top level nodes represent high-level motivational behaviors, such as "reproduction". The lowest level nodes correspond to simple sub-behaviors such as "lay eggs" and "comb feathers". There is a feeding of activation down through the hierarchy. Nodes in the same level inhibit one another so that only one can be active at any time. Lorenz [72] described a similar idea which emphasizes the effect of both internal and external stimuli in activating a specific behavior.

**Implementation Advantages.** Using a hierarchy to implement behavior arbitration offers certain advantages:

Handling Complexity and Conflict: Hierarchical structures are highly intuitive and hence easier to design and to diagnose. Very complex systems can be put together in a modular fashion. Additionally, in a hierarchy of behaviors, conflicts between them are greatly reduced by the more or less fixed priority preferences inherited in the structure.

Increasing Efficiency: Efficiency is obtained by information sharing. Knowledge obtained or processed by behaviors higher in the hierarchy can be used by behaviors lower in the hierarchy. For example, in the intention generator, when control flows down to the behavior 'eating', previously processed sensory information about surrounding obstacles (by the 'avoiding obstacle' behavior) can be used when the focusser is activated to compute the motor preferences (see the next section or Section 6.5.2) for performing the eating behavior.

Compared with distributed control structures, hierarchical control structures offer lower flexibility but higher controllability. In particular, hierarchical control involves a much smaller number of control parameters and hence makes it easy to converge to a desirable choice, while this is not necessarily true for distributed control.

## 7.6 Intention-Guided Perception: Control of the Focusser

As is described in the previous chapter, after the intention generator chooses an intention, it invokes the focusser. For example, when the *avoid* intention is generated, the perception focusser is activated to locate the positions of the obstacles, paying special attention to the most dangerous one. To enable the choice of favorable actions, the focusser must compute motor preferences in accordance with the environmental conditions (see Section. 6.5.3 for details). This process requires the availability of $\tau$ – the strength of the desire from which a motor preference was assigned a value. In the current implementation, motor preferences may be derived from four desires: avoid (collision), fear, eat and mate. Let $\tau^a$, $\tau^f$, $\tau^e$ and $\tau^m$ denote the strength of these four desires, respectively. Their values are given by:

$$\tau^a = 1.0,$$
$$\tau^f = F/\tau^I,$$
$$\tau^e = H/\tau^I,$$
$$\tau^m = L/\tau^I,$$

where $\tau^I$ ($I = \{e, a, f, m\}$) is the strength of the current intention and if $I \neq \{e, a, f, m\}$, $\tau^I = 1.0$.

Once the focusser has computed and collected all the motor preferences, it passes only information about the geometry, positions, and/or velocities of the attended object along with these preferences to the appropriate behavior routine.

## 7.7 Persistence in Behavior

In a complex dynamic world, an artificial fish should have some persistence in its behavior, especially in its intentions, otherwise it will tend to dither, perpetually changing its mind. Basic persistence in the behaviors is modeled implicitly by the intrinsic ranking (prioritization) between them, the continuity in the mental state variables, and the constancy of the habits. For instance, the collision avoidance behavior precedes all other behaviors and once invoked, will only terminate when the collision is cleared. Once the mental state of hunger is high enough to activate the feeding behavior, the continuity in $H$ (in particular the internal urge component) ensures that the activation level will not drop abruptly until the fish succeeds in taking more food. However, special attention needs to be paid to the maintenance of persistence in the case when an ongoing behavior is interrupted temporarily. In our case, there are two possible situations where an ongoing behavior may be interrupted: it may be interrupted by a behavior higher in the priority hierarchy triggered by some event or by an opportunity-triggered behavior.

### 7.7.1 Behavior Memory

If the current behavior is interrupted, the intention generator is able to store in a single-item short term memory (we do not wish to give artificial fish an unnaturally large memory capacity) the current intention and some associated information that may be used to resume the interrupted behavior. The typical use of this behavior memory is illustrated in Fig. 7.4. The persistence serves mainly to make longer duration behaviors such as feeding, mating and schooling more robust. Suppose for example that the current behavior is mating and that an imminent collision is detected. This causes an *avoid* intention and the storage of the *mate* intention (we refer to the stored intention as $I^s$ in Fig. 7.4) along with the identity of the mating partner. After the obstacle is cleared, the intention generator commands the focusser to generate up-to-date heading and range information about the mating partner, assuming it is still in viewing range. A similar scenario may occur during feeding. Moreover, feeding and mating can interrupt one another if appropriate opportunities present themselves.

### 7.7.2 Inhibitory Gain and Fatigue

To further ensure persistence in a behavior that has been interrupted and then resumed, we adopt the concept of *inhibitory gain* from ethology [114]. Inhibitory gain was first proposed by Ludlow to model the control mechanism in animals that balances persistence and opportunism. It is elicited by the winning behavior and is a negative value imposed on the activation energy (strength of desire) of all the competing behaviors. This helps to keep the activation of the winning behavior relatively high and hence induces persistence in that behavior. The higher the value of the inhibitory gain, the more persistent the behavior that releases it. In our case, since behaviors are layered in a hierarchy by their intrinsic priorities, the number of competing behaviors is reduced to those in the same layer rather than to all of the other behaviors had a distributed structure been used. The inhibitory gain $\delta = -0.2\tau$ (where $\tau$ is the activation value of the active behavior) is added to the competing behaviors only when the current behavior is one resumed from the behavior memory. Let us take the same example as above. When the mating behavior is resumed from the obstacle avoidance behavior, $\delta$ is added to $H$ to help maintain the persistence/continuity of the mating behavior by inhibiting further interruptions, say, from opportunistic feeding.

Excessive persistence in behavior can be undesirable in certain situations. For example, if we do not put food in the virtual marine world, a hungry fish would not engage in any behavior (in the same or lower priority layer) other than foraging. This can be avoided by modeling fatigue in behavior. Fatigue is also important for behavior time-sharing [96], in which low priority activities are given a chance to execute despite the presence of a higher priority activity. We model fatigue of a behavior by simply multiplying the corresponding activation value of that behavior with a decay function of time. A similar model of inhibitory gain and fatigue was proposed by Blumberg [115].

### 7.7.3 Persistence in Targeting

Different persistence can also be exhibited in the way an animal chooses its targets over time. Our design of the intention generator and focusser simplifies the modification of existing personalities and behaviors and the addition of new ones. For example, we can create artificial fishes with different persistences by augmenting the focusser with a positive valued threshold. Suppose the current intention of a predator fish is to *eat* and let the distance to some currently targeted prey be $l_c$ and the distance to some other prey be $l_n$. If $l_c - l_n$ is greater than the threshold, the fish will target the new prey. Varying the threshold will vary the fish's level of persistence. The same heuristic can be applied to mates when the fish is trying to *mate*. One can make the fish "fickle" by setting the value of the threshold close to zero or make it "devoted" by setting a large value.

## 7.8 Behavior Routines

Once the intention generator selects an intention, it attempts to satisfy the intention by passing control to a behavior routine along with the data from the perception focusser. The artificial fish currently includes nine behavior routines listed below plus five subroutines (listed within brackets below) which serve the obvious purposes:

1. *avoiding-static-obstacle*
2. *avoiding-fish*
3. *chasing-target*
4. *eating-food (suck-in)*
5. *mating (looping, circling, ascending, nuzzling)*
6. *leaving*
7. *wandering*
8. *escaping*
9. *schooling*

The activated behavior routine uses the focused perceptual data to select appropriate MCs and provide them with the proper motor control parameters. Note that more than one MC may be chosen if they are not mutually exclusive. For instance, swim-MC and ascend-MC can be selected simultaneously. We now briefly describe the function of the routines.

The *avoiding-static-obstacle* and *avoiding-fish* routines enable a fish to avoid potential collisions. The *chasing-target* routine guides a fish as it swims towards a goal. These more primitive, perception-driven behaviors are essential components of the more advanced motivational behaviors such as preying, schooling, and mating. We will give a more detailed description of these behaviors in the subsequent section.

The *eating-food* routine tests the distance $d$ from the fish's mouth to the targeted food (see Fig. 7.6). If $d$ is greater than some small threshold value, the routine *chasing-target* is invoked. When $d$ is less than the threshold value the subroutine *suck-in* is activated where a "vacuum" force (to be explained in Section 7.9.1) is calculated and then exerted on the food.

The *mating* routine invokes four subroutines: *looping, circling, ascending* and *nuzzling* (see Section 7.9.3 for details). The *wandering-about* routine sets the fish swimming at a certain speed by invoking the swim-MC, while sending random turn angles to the turn-MCs intermittently. The *leaving* routine is similar to the *wandering-about* routine. The *escaping* routine chooses suitable MCs according to the relative position, orientation of the predator to the fish. The *schooling* routine will be discussed in Section 7.9.2.

### 7.8.1 Primitive Behavior: Avoiding Potential Collisions

Collision avoidance is one of the most important and most commonly performed behaviors in all animals. Once the artificial fish's perception system detects a potential collision (see Section 6.6.1), it immediately acts to avoid it. Collision avoidance with a static obstacle and with another fish are implemented by the behavior routines *avoiding-static-obstacle* and *avoiding-fish*, respectively. They operate in much the same way: Given the relative position of an obstacle, an appropriate action (e.g. left-turn-MC) is chosen subject to the motor preferences imposed by other surrounding stimuli. Then the proper control parameters for the chosen motor skill(s), such as the speed and angle of turn, are calculated using the sensory information about that obstacle as well as available motor preferences.

For efficiency the *avoiding-fish* routine treats the dynamic obstacle as a rectangular bounding box moving in a certain direction. Although collisions between fish cannot always be avoided, bounding boxes can easily be adjusted such that they almost always are, and the method is efficient.

### 7.8.2 Primitive Behavior: Moving Target Pursuit

To enable an artificial fish to follow a moving target, we have implemented a routine *chasing-target*. This routine plays a crucial role in several higher-level behavior routines such as mating.

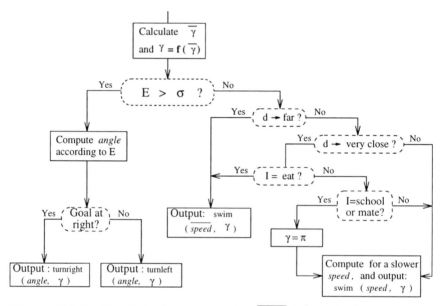

**Figures 7.5.** Outline of *chasing-target* routine. $\overline{speed}$ denotes the fastest swimming speed of an artificial fish

Fig. 7.5 outlines the *chasing-target*($\mathbf{g}$, $I$, $\sigma$) routine, where $\mathbf{g}$ (Fig. 7.6) is the 3D position of the target in the fish's local coordinate system , $I$ is an integer indexing the fish's current intention, and $0 \le \sigma < \pi/2$ is a threshold angle indicating how closely in direction (orientation) the fish should follow the target. The closeness is measured by $E$ where $0 \le E \le \pi$ is the angle between the fish's orientation $X_f$ and the projection of $\mathbf{g}$ onto the local $X_f Y_f$-plane (Fig. 7.6). In most cases (i.e. when $I = mate$, $I = leave$, and $I = school$), $\sigma$ is a nonzero constant (e.g. $\sigma = \pi/5$ when $I = school$) so that the fish can quickly approach the target in roughly the right direction rather

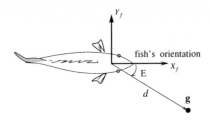

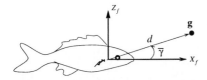

**Figures 7.6.** The position of target **g** relative to the fish: characterized by angle $E$, angle $\bar{\gamma}$ and distance $d$

than spending most of its time steering without making much progress. When $I = eat$, $\sigma$ is given according to the distance $d$ to the target ($d = \|\mathbf{g}\|$). In general, when the target is far away (i.e. $d$ is greater than a threshold value), $\sigma$ is relatively large so that the fish can rapidly home into the target. When the target is near, $\sigma$ decreases to provide more targeting accuracy.

The output of *chasing-target* is the activation of one of the following muscle motor controllers:

- swim-MC(speed)
- right-turn-MC(angle)
- left-turn-MC(angle)

along with the activation of one of the pectoral fin motor controllers:

- ascend-MC($\gamma$)
- descend-MC($\gamma$)
- brake-MC($\gamma = \pi$)

The speed parameter is set based upon the distance $d$, such that the fish swims at full speed when the target is far, and in order to gain more control over steering, slows down as it approaches the target. The fin angle control parameter $\gamma$ is calculated from the up-down angle $\bar{\gamma}$ (Fig. 7.6):

$$\gamma = f(\bar{\gamma}) = \begin{cases} \bar{\gamma} + \pi/2 & \text{if } |\bar{\gamma}| \le \pi/4 \\ 3\pi/4 & \text{if } \bar{\gamma} > \pi/4 \\ \pi/4 & \text{if } \bar{\gamma} < -\pi/4 \end{cases}$$

When $\bar{\gamma} > 0$, the ascend-MC is invoked and when $\bar{\gamma} < 0$, the descend-MC is invoked. When braking is needed in the schooling or mating behaviors, the brake-MC is invoked.

Furthermore, when $I = eat$ the angle parameters of the turn-MCs are calculated by taking into account the velocity with which the target moves. For example, consider the case when the target is located to the right of the fish and is moving to the right. Suppose that $E > \sigma$ and the matching set of motor control parameters for $E$ from the steering map is $P_E$ (see Fig. 4.9), then, to anticipate the movement of the target, $P_{E+\delta E}$ (obtained by a right shift from $E$), rather than $P_E$, is output to indicate an 'overshot turn'. The amount of the shift is proportional to the speed with which the target is traveling. This maneuver, observed in predatory animals when pursuing a prey, is referred to as 'interception' by ethologists [116].

**Figures 7.7.** A peaceful marine world. See the original color image in Appendix D

**Figures 7.8.** The smell of danger. See the original color image in Appendix D

## 7.9 Artificial Fish Types

Three types of artificial fishes have been implemented – predators, prey, and pacifists. This section presents their implementation details. Fig. 7.7 shows pacifist fishes in a peaceful marine world. Fig. 7.8 shows a large (dark colored) predator pursuing a small prey fish.

### 7.9.1 Predators

Fig. 7.9 is a schematic of the intention generator of a predator, which is a specialized version of Fig. 7.4. To simplify matters, currently predators are not preyed upon by other predators, so they perform no predator detection, and *escape*, *school*, and *mate* intentions are disabled ($F = 0$, $L = 0$). Since predators cruise perpetually, the *leave* intention is also disabled.

Generally potential prey are in less danger of being hunted when they are far away from the predator, or are in a school, or are behind the predator. A predator chases prey $k$ if the cost of reaching it is minimal. This idea is

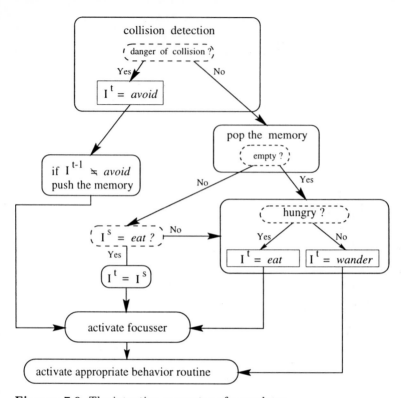

**Figures 7.9.** The intention generator of a predator

based on the *optimal foraging theory* in ethology, which in its original form states that when an animal is feeding it makes its decisions in such a way that it will maximize its net rate of energy intake [16]. We model the cost of feeding on prey $k$ as $C_k = d_k(1 + \beta_1 S_k + \beta_2 E_k/\pi)$, where $d_k$ is the distance between the mouth of the predator and the center of prey $k$'s body, $S_k = 1$ if prey $k$ is in a school of fishes, otherwise $S_k = 0$, and the angle $E_k \in [0, \pi)$ (Fig. 7.10 and Fig. 4.11) measures the turning cost. $\beta_1$ and $\beta_2$ are parameters that tune the contributions of $S_k$ and $E_k$. We use $\beta_1 = 0.5$ and $\beta_2 = 0.2$ in our implementation of the focusser.

**Ingestion.** Most teleost fishes do not bite on their victims like sharks do [117]. When a fish is about to eat it swims close to the victim and extends its protrusile jaw, thus creating a hollow space within the mouth. The pressure difference between the inside and the outside of the mouth produces a vacuum force that sucks into the mouth the victim and anything else in the nearby water. The predator closes its mouth, expels the water through the gills, and grinds the food with pharyngeal jaws [24]. We simulate this process by enabling the artificial fish to open and close its mouth kinematically. When it wants to suck in prey, it opens its mouth and, while the mouth is open, exerts

Predator

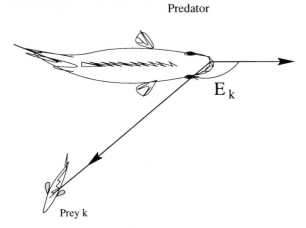

$E_k$

Prey k

**Figures 7.10.** The angle $E_k$.

vacuum forces on nearby fishes and other dynamic particles in the vicinity of the open mouth, drawing them in. The vacuum forces are added to external nodal forces $\mathbf{f}_i$ in Eq. (4.2). Fig. 7.11 shows a predator fish ingesting prey fish.

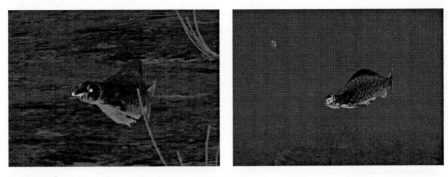

**Figures 7.11.** A hungry predator ingesting prey

### 7.9.2 Prey

The intention generator of a prey fish is a specialization of the generic intention generator of Fig. 7.4 as shown in Fig. 7.12. The two characteristic behaviors of prey fish are schooling and evading predators. We briefly present the implementation of the two behaviors.

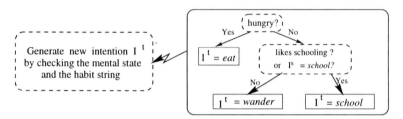

**Figures 7.12.** Portion of intention generator of prey

Schooling is a complex behavior where all the fishes swim in generally the same direction (see Fig. 7.14a). Each fish constantly adjusts its speed and direction to match those of other members of the school. They maintain a certain distance from one another, roughly one body length from neighbors on average [24]. Each member of a school of artificial fish acts autonomously, and the schooling behavior is achieved through sensory perception and locomotion [9]. An inceptive school is formed when a few fish swim towards a lead fish (see Fig. 7.14b). Once a fish is in some proximity to some other schooling fish, the 'schooling' behavior routine outlined in Fig. 7.13 is invoked.

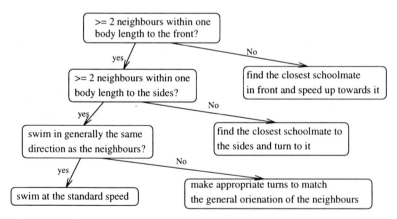

**Figures 7.13.** Schooling behavior routine

The intention generator ensures that the fish do not get too close together, because the *avoid* collision intention has highest precedence. To create more compact schools, the collision sensitivity region of a schooling fish is decreased once the fish gets into formation. When a large school encounters an obstacle, the autonomous obstacle avoidance behavior of individual fishes may cause the school to split into two groups (obstacle avoidance behavior has higher priority than the schooling behavior). Once the obstacle is cleared, the behavior memory of individual fishes ensures that the *schooling* behavior routine regains control and hence the school rejoins (Fig. 7.15(a)-(d)).

Similar to the flocking of boids [9], the *schooling* behavior of artificial fish is achieved through the interaction of two behaviors – to stay in the neighborhood of other schooling fish (by using *chasing-target*) and to avoid being too close to any of them (by invoking *avoiding-fish*). Each fish acts independently based on its perception of its neighborhood. One can adjust the density of a school by adjusting the collision sensitivity regions of the schooling fish (Fig. 6.8(b)). For instance, increasing the sensitivity region can create more loosely coupled schools. In our implementation, there is a designated 'leader fish' that swims in front of all other fish in the school. The general path that the school takes is determined by the leader fish. Of course, the leader fish could also be decided dynamically at run time, i.e. whichever fish is frontmost will become the leader.

When a predator gets too close to any fish the *escaping* behavior is triggered. This examines the relative position between the fish and the predator against a set of rules. Each rule suggests a proper action in a certain situation. For example, *If predator is closely behind and swims in roughly the same direction and is to the right of fish, then turn to the left.* One may consider all these rules as the specifications of one general rule, that is, to swim away from the predator as fast as possible. Rules are interpreted as detailed geometrical/mathematical conditions, and their quantities determine the values of motor control parameters such as the angle of a turn. Currently there are eleven rules and the resulting behavior looks natural. Fig. 7.16a and 7.16b show two instances of a small school of prey scattering in terror when a predator comes close. Note how each of the prey fish tries independently to flee from the pursuing predator.

The eleven rules based on which a prey fish flees from a predator are listed below (note "me" or "mine" indicate the fleeing prey fish):

## if predator is far:

- *if* predator is in front, *then* turn 180 degrees;
- *else if* predator is behind, *then* proceed at full speed;
- *else if* predator is to the left side, *then* turn right;
- *else if* predator is to the right side, *then* turn left;

**Figures 7.14a.** A small school of angelfish

**Figures 7.14b.** An inceptive school

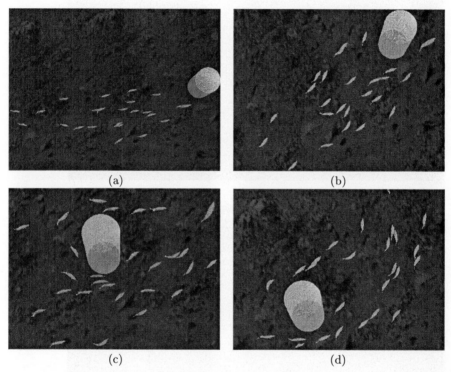

(a)                                          (b)

(c)                                          (d)

**Figures 7.15.** A school of fish encounters an obstacle, splits, and rejoins after it has cleared the obstacle

**Figures 7.16a.** School scatters in terror

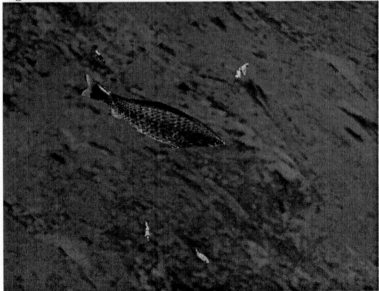

**Figures 7.16b.** Fleeing from predator

**if predator is close:**

- If predator is in front:
  - *if* predator's heading is roughly perpendicular to mine, *then*:
    - *if* predator is heading towards my left side, *then* turn right;
    - *else* turn left;
  - *else* turn 180 degrees;
- Else if predator is behind:
  - *if* predator's heading is roughly the same as mine and is approaching, *then*:
    - *if* predator is to the left, *then* turn right;
    - *else* turn left;
  - *else if* predator's heading is roughly perpendicular to mine, *then*:
    - *if* predator is heading towards my left side, *then* turn right;
    - *else* turn left;
  - *else* proceed at full speed;
- Else if predator is to the side:
  - *if* predator is to the left, *then* turn right;
  - *else* turn left;

### 7.9.3 Pacifists

The intention generator of a pacifist differs from that of a prey in that intention *mate* is enabled and the intentions *escape* and *school* are disabled. Piscatorial mating behaviors show great interspecies and intra-species diversity [118]. However, two behaviors are prevalent: (i) nuzzling, where typically the male approaches the female from underneath and nudges her abdomen repeatedly until she is ready to spawn, and (ii) spawning ascent, where in its simplest form, the female rapidly swims towards the surface pursued by the male and releases gametes at the peak of her ascent. Moreover, courtship dancing is common in many species, albeit with substantial variation. Two frequently observed patterns are looping, in which the male swims vigorously up and down in a loop slightly above and in front of the female, and circling, in which the male and female circle, seemingly chasing each other's tail. Fig. 7.17a shows photographs of natural fish displaying various mating behaviors [118].

The complex mating rituals observed in the majority of animals are composed of a sequence of sub-behaviors (e.g. courting, spawning ascent) performed in a unique order. This is referred to as *fixed action patterns* by ethologists [93]. We have implemented a *mating* behavior routine which simulates courtship looping, circling, spawning ascent, and nuzzling in sequence (see Fig. 7.18 and Fig. 7.9.3(a)-(f)). This sequence is represented as a finite-state machine where each state is linked with a component behavior and has a boolean transition function. The transition function evaluates the associated

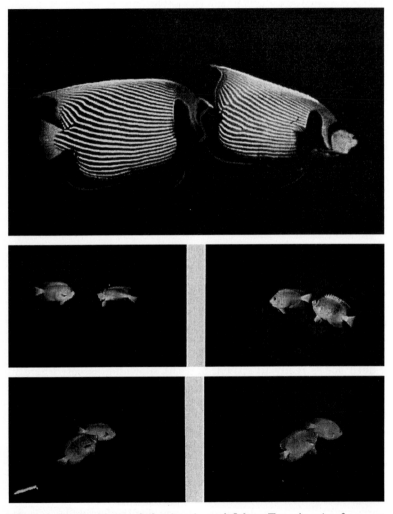

**Figures 7.17a.** Mating behaviors in real fishes. Top: A pair of emperor angelfish are ascending to spawn, the male is behind and slightly below the female. Middle-left: A pair of *C. interruptus* engaged in mutual courting. Middle-right: Spawning ascent of the pair. Bottom: Instances of nuzzling behavior. (Reproduced from the book by Thresher [118])

behavior to see if it is completed, if positive, a transition is performed and the next component behavior is activated.

A male fish selects a mating partner based on the following criteria: A female of the same species is more attractive than one of different species, and closer females are more attractive than ones further away. A female selects a partner similarly, but shows preference to male fish size (stronger, more protective) rather than proximity. Suppose some fish $i$ has selected a potential partner $j$ then one of three things may happen:

Fish $j$'s intention is not to mate:    Fish $i$ approaches $j$ and follows it around by performing the *chasing-target* behavior.

Fish $j$'s intention is to mate but not with fish $i$:    If $i$ is female it will choose another potential mate. Otherwise $i$ is male and it will perform *looping* behavior in front of $j$ for a certain amount of time. If $j$ is suitably impressed during this time period then she will select $i$ and the courtship sequence continues, otherwise $i$ will discontinue *looping* and *leave* $j$ to find a new potential partner. Fig. 7.18 shows two examples where two male poker fish vying for the attention of a female by performing elaborate looping behavior.

Fish $j$'s intention is to mate with fish $i$:    *Courtship* behavior starts with the male looping in front of the female while she hovers and bobs her head. The female's hovering and head bobbing is accomplished through motor control of her pectoral fins.

The male looping behavior is simulated by invoking *chasing-target*, with the 'target' being a point in front of the female's head which moves up and down at a certain frequency. When the number of times that the male reaches the moving point exceeds a certain threshold he makes a transition from *looping* to *circling* behavior. Although the threshold is fixed, in practice the actual motions and duration of looping is highly unpredictable due to any number of reasons, such as looping being temporarily suspended to avoid a collision. If a new larger male joins in the *looping* display before the transition to *circling*, then the female may reject her initial partner and turn to the new fish. The rejected male will then turn away as described in the second case, above.

The *circling* behavior is implemented using *chasing-target*, where the target is the other fishes tail and is completed after the female has made a fixed number of turns. Next the spawning *ascending* routine is invoked whereby the female fish ascends quickly upwards and then hovers. She is followed by the male who uses *chasing-target* to follow her abdomen. In the *nuzzling* behavior routine, the male approaches her abdomen from below until he successfully touches it with his mouth. He then retreats, waits, and repeats the process. For such close contact to occur both fish's collision sensitivity region is set very close to their bodies.

**Figures 7.18.** Two males (larger) vying for the attention of a female

## 7.10 Discussion

In this section we examine the properties of our action selection mechanism against a set of criteria commonly accepted by researchers in designing animats. Possible extensions of our current implementation are also discussed.

### 7.10.1 Analysis

The set of design criteria for effective action selection mechanisms listed in the beginning of this chapter can also be used to evaluate the effectiveness of an action selection mechanism. Next, we examine the properties of our design of the artificial fish's behavior system against each of those criteria and present the result.

**Priority of Different Behaviors.** The priorities of the range of behaviors we have emulated are implemented by the hierarchical structure of the intention generator. Life-preserving behaviors (collision avoidance, escape from predators) are guaranteed to take precedence over other behaviors. Behaviors at the same priority level in the hierarchy, such as eating and mating, are further prioritized by the dynamics of the corresponding desires.

**Persistence in Behavior.** Persistence in behavior is achieved by the use of the simple memory, and the modeling of inhibitory gain and fatigue described in Section 7.7.

**Compromised Actions.** Compromised actions are enabled in the behavior system via the use of motor preferences. This design is considerably more efficient than that of a free-flow hierarchy [91]. In a free-flow hierarchy, every behavior must compute a recommendation for the next action. There will be no winner until all of the recommendations arrive at the motor command level, where a winning action is decided by fusing all the recommendations

(a): Angelfish looping

(b): Angelfish Circling

(c): Angelfish Ascending

(d): Angelfish Nuzzling

(e): Clownfish Circling

(f): Clownfish Nuzzling

(see Appendix C.2 for more detail about free-flow hierarchy). While a free-flow hierarchy pays no special attention to the most desirable behavior given the current situation, our design of the intention generator takes the opposite approach. It picks a winning behavior at an early stage such that irrelevant sensory information need not be processed. This reflects the advantages of a winner-takes-all selection process. However, unlike a conventional winner-takes-all process, the use of the motor preferences allows unselected behaviors to influence *how* the winning behavior is performed. We believe that our implementation is a good compromise between efficiency and functionality.

Moreover, the qualitative nature of the motor preferences simplifies both the process of generating them and the way of using them (see Section 6.5.3). This is in direct contrast to the quantitative action recommendations used in Tyrrell's implementation. Merging the recommendations into a single motor command was shown by Tyrrell to be a complicated and difficult problem even when all the actions are specified in a 2D discrete world. It will thus be even more problematic if the actions are defined in a 3D continuous world. In addition, it is doubtful that most animals make their decisions to act by carefully evaluating and optimizing all possible actions. For this reason, using qualitative motor preferences seems to be more biologically plausible.

**Opportunism.** Opportunism is enabled through explicit modeling of the effect of external stimulus on the mental state variables (Section 7.4). Fig. 7.19 shows a clownfish, previously engaged in mating rituals, takes an opportunity to eat the nearby plankton.

**Figures 7.19.** A clownfish displays opportunism in behavior

**Real-Valued Sensory Readings.** In addition, real-valued sensory readings (as opposed to binary predicates) have been used throughout the design of the behavior system. The particular form of sensory information passed from the perception to the behavior system affects how effectively the behavior system couples perception to action. We believe that real-valued sensory readings are more convenient to use especially when deriving motor control parameters for specifying continuous 3D actions. The convincing animation results we have been able to obtain demonstrates the success of using real-valued sensory information. Binary sensory readings may be sufficient for behavior arbitration in a virtual environment with modest complexity as is shown by Maes [81]. (For more details about Maes' implementation, see Appendix C.1.) However, Maes' mechanism does not consider how a chosen behavior can be implemented, which disregards half of the action selection process.

## 7.10.2 Summary

We have demonstrated the soundness of the design of the artificial fish's behavior system. Although arbitrarily more complex designs could be conceived and implemented with additional effort, our current design is sufficient for its purpose. That is to say, we have established a computational model of animal behavior, that can be effectively used for computer animation and, can serve as a touchstone for developing ALife theory.

It should be realized that, although we have validated the behavior control scheme (see Fig. 7.2) via an artificial fish agent, a scheme such as ours is by no means restricted to the control of fish behavior. Rather, the aspects of behavior captured in our model, i.e. perception, internal motivation, external stimuli and how they interact to produce intentions and to select actions, are generally applicable to all animals. This suggests many potential extensions of our behavior control scheme to the modeling of other creatures. This is best demonstrated by the work of Blumberg and Galyean [119], where a behavior control paradigm similar to ours, was used to direct the behavior of a kinematic graphical dog creature.

On the one hand we realize that a crucial step in our behavior control scheme is the construction of effective motor controllers. Realistic visual effects depend on how well the motor controllers can control the underlying model of the animal, to produce realistic locomotion. On the other hand, abstracting motor controllers is a necessary step towards the modeling of higher level behaviors. Currently, motor control in complex creatures, such as articulated figures, remains an unsolved problem. However when the underlying control problem for such creatures is solved, we believe the design of our behavioral control scheme can provide the starting point for the modeling of the behaviors of the animal in question. Thus, as we have stated in Chapter 2, the unavailability of motor controllers for a particular animal, should not imply a lack of generality of the control scheme we have proposed.

For animals that have complex cognitive abilities, additional control layers may be added on top of the current control scheme. The current control scheme can serve as a reactive behavioral control layer for the more basic behaviors of the animal, such as collision avoidance, foraging and mating. Moreover, many higher animals possess actuators (e.g. limbs) that are beyond the necessity of locomotion, for example, the arms and hands of primates and humans. These actuators may provide a large number of motor skills relevant to manipulation which are mutually exclusive to those used for locomotion. Consequently, the chances of being able to fulfill more than one intention at a time are greatly increased. This suggests that it may be advantageous to permit multiple intentions to be active simultaneously. For instance, a synthetic human actor should be able to fulfill both the intention of searching for someone in a crowded room and the intention of not spilling a cup of coffee.

Let us consider drawing a spectrum of various behavior control schemes, with the strictly winner-takes-all and the free-flow selection processes occupying the two extremes. It is reasonable to assume that a desirable control scheme would be a compromise between the extremes. In particular, such a scheme should allow multiple intentions to be active simultaneously while still maintaining reasonable simulation speed. This can be done by restricting the allowable number of active intentions. In addition, in order to generate behavior-oriented, harmonic movements, a more elaborate fusion mechanism at the motor level would be necessary to collect and combine the resulting motor commands.

# 8. Modeling the Marine Environment

To enhance the visual realism of the marine environment, we have created physics-based animate models of seaweeds, plankton, and water currents.

## 8.1 Water Current

In the current implementation, we simulate a simple fluid flow field using techniques similar to the ones used by Wejchert and Haumann [45] for animating aerodynamics. Assuming inviscid and irrotational fluid, we can construct a model of a non-turbulent flow field with low computational cost using a set of *flow primitives*. These include *uniform flow* where the fluid velocity follow straight lines; *source flow* – a point from which fluid moves out from all directions; *sink flow* which is opposite to the source flow; and *vortex flow* where fluid moves around in concentric circles (see Fig. 8.1). More complicated flow fields can be constructed by combining different flow primitives.

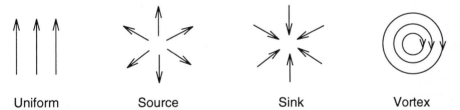

| Uniform | Source | Sink | Vortex |

**Figures 8.1.** The flow primitives (reproduced from the paper by Wejchert and Haumann[45])

The fluid flow field in our implementation consists of a uniform flow with sinusoidal strength and a source flow at each cylindrical obstacle. The velocity field of the uniform flow is $\mathbf{v}^u = a\,\sin(\omega t)\mathbf{v}$, where $a$ is a positive real-valued parameter that represents the maximal strength of the flow; $\omega$ is a parameter angle and $t$ is the animation time step – together they define the 'cycle' time of the uniform flow; $\mathbf{v}$ is the unit vector indicating the orientation of the uniform flow. The source flow velocity field (i.e., the flow velocity at a point whose 3D coordinates are given by $\mathbf{v}^s$) at cylinder $C$ is defined as:

$$\mathbf{v}^s = \begin{cases} \frac{a}{(d-r)^2}\mathbf{d} & \text{if point } \mathbf{v}^s \text{ is lower than the height of } C \\ 0 & \text{otherwise} \end{cases}$$

where $d$ is the shortest distance from point $\mathbf{v}^s$ to the center line of the source (or axis of $C$), $r$ is the radius of $C$ and $\mathbf{d}$ is the unit vector along $d$ pointing outward from the center of the source. The source flow fields are added to the uniform flow field in order to approximate the effect of fluid flowing around obstacles [45].

Note that in Eq. (4.3), the influence of the flow field on the fish's locomotion is taken into account by using the relative velocity between the surface and the fluid. In direct contrast to using non-physics-based models, here subtle locomotional behaviors exhibited when fish swim upstream or downstream or being buffeted by water currents can be easily modeled in a physically plausible way.

## 8.2 Seaweeds, Plankton and Air Bubbles

The dynamic seaweeds respond to simulated water currents in a realistic manner. Each leaf of a seaweed cluster is a mass-spring chain. The springs have identical spring constants, but the distance between mass points as well as the mass of the successive nodes decreases from the root to the tip (thus the leaf is more flexible and lighter towards the tip). The leaves have positive buoyancy in the virtual water and they are subject to the simulated currents which cause them to sway. In order to obtain computational efficiency, we do not calculate the forces acting on the geometric surface of each seaweed leaf, rather, we approximate the hydrodynamic force at each mass point as $\mathbf{f}_i = \mu_w \mathbf{v}$, where $\mu_w$ is the fluid viscosity defined in Eq. (4.3) and $\mathbf{v}$ is the aggregate fluid velocity $\mathbf{v}^u + \mathbf{v}^s$ at mass point $i$.

Fig. 8.2 shows a sequence of snapshots of the swaying motion of a seaweed cluster (the simulated water currents are as described above). In addition, when a fish swims through or passes by a seaweed, the leaves respond to a simulated water force generated by the fish's body. Fig. 8.3 shows how the leaves close to the fish's body are "pushed" away by the simulated hydrodynamic forces caused by the fish. The plankton are simply modeled as floating mass points under the influence of the simulated water currents. Using the same principle, we have also modeled air bubbles rising from the seafloor to the surface of water.

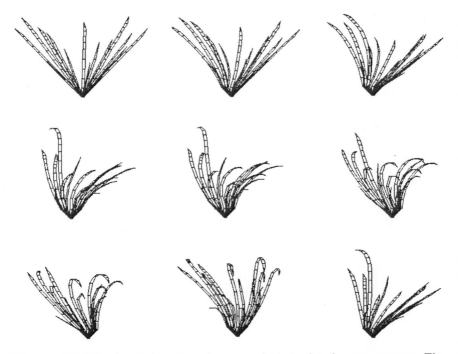

**Figures 8.2.** The swaying motion of a seaweed in simulated water currents. The image in the upper left corner shows the leaves at their initial rest position

**Figures 8.3.** The seaweed responds to hydrodynamic forces produced by a passing fish

# 9. The Graphical User Interface

In this chapter we describe the graphical user interface that we have developed for our animation system. The purpose of the user interface is to make it easy for the animator to initialize animations and to control the behaviors of the artificial fishes at the low level, i.e., the physics level, and at the high level, i.e., the motivation level. We implemented the interface using the *Forms Library* [120].

## 9.1 Initialization Panels

Currently, there are two panels that facilitate the creation of virtual marine worlds. The first panel, shown in Fig. 9.1, lets the animator select the numbers of different objects in the animation and is used in the beginning of an animation. The available selections include eight species of fish (corresponding to eight different textures), and three environmental items: plankton, seaweeds and obstacle cylinders. The user can select an item and input the desired number of the item from the keyboard. With a companion pop-up panel, the user can specify the number of leaves in each seaweed cluster. It is also possible to read all the necessary data from a script file by pressing the "scriptfile" button and specifying the file name.

The second panel, shown in Fig. 9.2, lets the animator initialize the positions of objects in an animation. The user is able to move around and re-size individual objects and observe the result in the graphics window. Once the user is satisfied with the current layout and setting, she/he can then save it as a script file for later use.

## 9.2 Manipulation Panels

The interface also provides to the animator the ability to manipulate the physical parameters of the underlying physics-based fish model as well as its behavioral parameters. This in turn enables an animator to direct the fish's behavior to a certain degree.

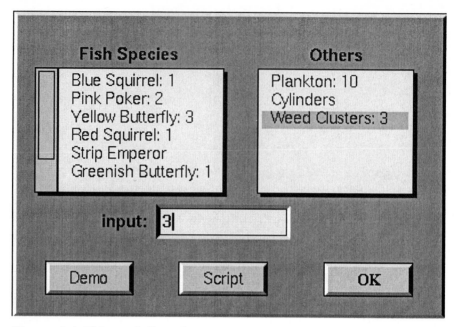

**Figures 9.1.** This panel allows the user to set the numbers of objects in the virtual marine world

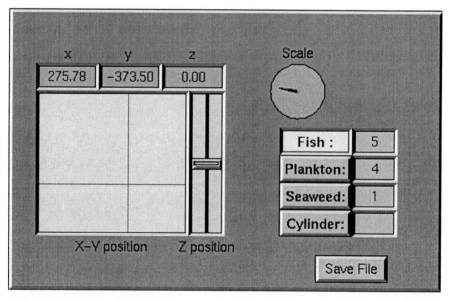

**Figures 9.2.** This panel allows the user to initialize the positions and sizes of objects in the virtual marine world

**Experimenting with the Physics.** Fig. 9.3 shows the interface through which the user can experiment with the physical and numerical attributes of the artificial fish model. The overall mass of the fish can be varied by changing the unit mass, i.e. using the "UnitMass" slider. The viscosity constant $\kappa_i$ can be altered by using the "Visco" slider. Similarly, the user is able to vary the spring constants and the fluid viscosity factor $\mu_w$ (in Eq. (4.3). The user can then determine how these parameters affect the motion of the artificial fish. The user can also turn off the hydrodynamic forces and see how a fish beats its tail without moving, and gradually loses its balance and stability and may finally become numerically unstable and "explode". Using the positioner, the user can specify the direction of the simulated uniform water currents. The effect of the water currents on the motions of the artificial fishes can be switched on or off by using the "Current(On/Off)" button. In addition, the user can change the integration time step to test the basic stability of the numerical solver and also to change the number of iterations per display to control the temporal sampling rate of the animation.

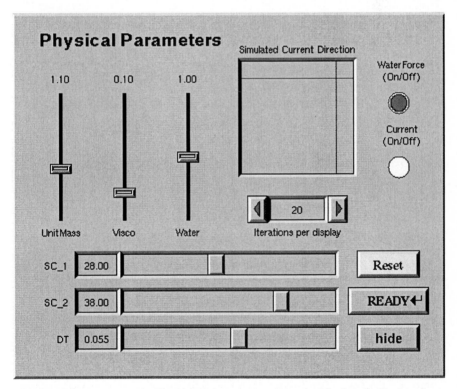

**Figures 9.3.** This panel allows the user to experiment with the physical and numerical parameters of the dynamic fish model

**Influencing a Fish's Behavior.** The animator can influence each fish's behavior at the motivation level by varying the relevant behavioral parameters in its mental state variables through the behavior panel (see Fig. 9.4) and by changing its habits through the habit panel (see Fig. 9.5). Using the behavior panel, the animator can also view the dynamics of the mental state of a chosen fish and its current intention. A fish's habit is implemented as a binary string with '1' representing 'like' and '0' representing 'dislike'. If two conflicting features are both assigned '1', for example, if both 'cold' and 'hot' buttons are pushed, this is taken to mean 'don't care'. The fish is a female if 'sex' equals '1'.

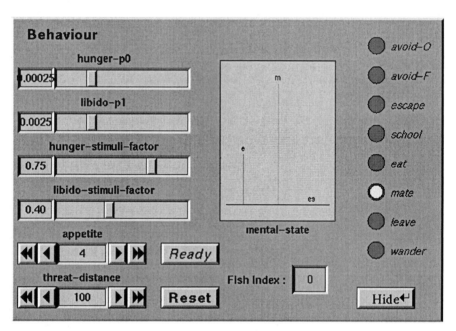

**Figures 9.4.** The behavior panel. The user can vary the behavioral parameters shown by the sliders. The chart shows the time-varying values of the fish's mental state variables (here the libido of fish '0' is the highest) and the lit round button indicates that the current intention is to mate

## 9.3 Control Panels

There is a general control panel (see Fig. 9.6) where all the previously mentioned panels reside as pop-up icons. There are also a set of additional buttons for controlling various graphical attributes, such as different rendering modes, or for turning on and off certain features, such as drawing the indices of the

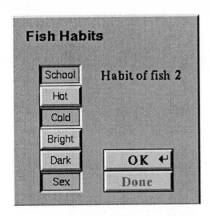

**Figures 9.5.** The habit panel is used to set a chosen fish's habits. Here, fish '2' is initialized to be female, to like schooling and cold temperature, and to not care about brightness of the environment

fishes. Moreover, the user is able to push buttons to output certain data, such as the camera angles, or to dump the current graphics window into an image file, etc.

When the "Fish View" button is pushed, a fishview control panel (see Fig. 9.7) pops up, allowing the user to select to view binocular retinal images from a chosen fish's point of view. Slider "pan" gives the gaze angle specifying the horizontal rotation of the eyeball and slider "tilt" gives the gaze angle specifying the vertical rotation of the eyeball. The retinal images are normally rendered as if the fish is looking in the direction of swimming (pan = 0 and tilt = 0), but the user can 'interfere' by manipulating "pan" and "tilt" to get different views. The retinal identity maps mentioned in Section 6.7 (see Fig. 6.9a) can be rendered on command by pressing the "ID map" button.

## 9.4 Discussion

The current implementation of the user interface is rather basic. We would like to enhance it in the future by adding new features. In particular, we would like to be able to directly control the behavior of a particular fish through the interface. For example, this would allow the user to "become" one of the artificial fishes, to look through the fish's eyes, and explore the virtual marine world. Or the user may be able to don a VR suit and become a virtual scuba diver swimming among artificial fish and eliciting their responses by, say, feeding them, etc.

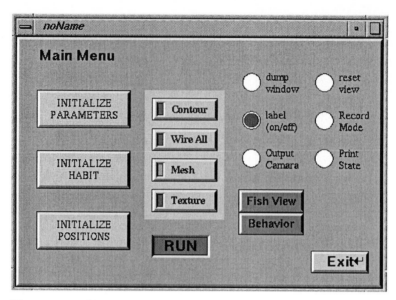

**Figures 9.6.** The general control panel

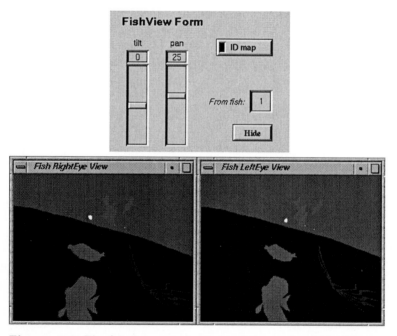

**Figures 9.7.** The fishview control panel and the rendered identity maps from the eyes of a particular fish (fish '1')

# 10. Animation Results

The visual results of the research described in this dissertation are captured in a number of short animation clips and two mini animation films "Go Fish!" and "A National Geo-Graphics Society Special: The Undersea World of Jack Cousto". "Go Fish!" was made in 1993 and was selected and presented at the ACM SIGGRAPH'93 Electronic Theater Evening Program [25]. "The Undersea World of Jack Cousto" was made in 1994 and was presented at the ACM SIGGRAPH'95 Electronic Theater Evening Program. Both animations were subsequently broadcast in various television science programs internationally.[1] "Go Fish!" has also won several awards, including the 1994 *Canadian Academy of Multimedia and Arts and Sciences International Award for Technical Excellence.* In the following sections, we briefly describe "Go Fish!" and "The Undersea World of Jack Cousto", as well as the contents of some additional animation shorts.

## 10.1 "Go Fish!"

"Go Fish!" runs for two minutes and four seconds and was produced by the author along with her supervisors, Professor Demetri Terzopoulos and Professor Eugene Fiume.

The animation first illustrates the construction of a dynamic fish model. The mass-spring-damper biomechanical substructure with its 12 primary contractile muscles is simulated in real time. The substructure is then enclosed in a realistically shaped NURBS surface to create the fish body. The fish surface is texture mapped using textures extracted from photographs of real fishes.

Next we see the simulated foraging behaviors of a small school of wire-frame fish among cylindrical obstacles. We are also treated to a fisheye ("fish-cam") view of the virtual aquatic world.

The final sequence shows a colorful variety of fish feeding in translucent water. In the presence of underwater currents, the fishes explore their world as autonomous agents, foraging for edible plankton and navigating around

---

[1] The interested reader is referred to the author's home page http://www.dgp.toronto.edu/people/tu for a list of programs in which the two animations were shown.

fixed and moving obstacles such as other fishes and dynamic seaweeds that grow from the sea bed. A sharp hook on a line descends towards the fish. A hapless fish, the first to bite the bait, is caught and pulled to the surface. The following images show stills from the animation which was rendered using the Silicon Graphics GL graphics library.

**Figures 10.1.** Denizens of the virtual marine world happily feeding on plankton

## 10.2 "The Undersea World of Jack Cousto"

The French oceanographer Jacques Cousteau has become legendary for his spectacular cinematography of natural marine life. The reader may be familiar with the magnificent underwater documentaries produced by the *Jacques Cousteau Foundation* or those of the *National Geographic Society*.

We have implemented an animation system that enables an animator to produce intriguing "nature documentaries" of an artificial undersea world, not by conventional means, but by assuming the role of a marine cinematographer analogous to that played by Cousteau. Unlike Cousteau, however, who must deal with a physical camera in a physical world, our animator uses a virtual camera to explore and record artificial life inhabiting a virtual marine world. To demonstrate this new gender of computer animation, we

**Figures 10.2.** Hungry fishes approaching the hook

**Figures 10.3.** A hapless fish is caught and pulled to the surface. See the original color image in Appendix D

have created a mini animated parody of a National Geographic underwater documentary.

Our "National Geo-Graphics" documentary explores "The Undersea World of Jack Cousto". Jack's cinematography reveals a mysterious world of colorful artificial fishes. We observe mating rituals and other elaborate behaviors. Dangerous predators stalk in the deceptively peaceful habitat. The following images show stills from the animation, which was rendered using the photorealistic RenderMan$^{TM}$ package.

"The Undersea World of Jack Cousto" runs for two minutes and thirty seconds and was produced by the author along with her colleague Radek Grzeszczuk and Professor Demetri Terzoupoulos.

**Figures 10.4.** A dangerous shark stalking a school of prey

## 10.3 Animation Short: Preying Behavior

At the beginning of the animation, the 'food chain' phenomenon of a small underwater ecosystem is displayed: various species of colorful 'pacifist' fishes are happily feeding on floating plankton (food particles) while a ferocious predator fish is stalking a prey fish, hoping to devour it. The remainder of the animation demonstrates the hunting behavior of the predator and the evasive behavior of the prey. We see the greedy predator chasing after each

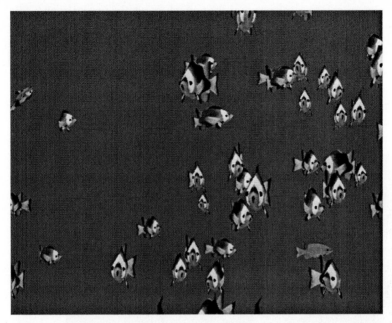

**Figures 10.5.** A school of fleeing prey. See the original color image in Appendix D

**Figures 10.6.** A pair of courting pokerfish. The male is on the right

prey until the prey is in close proximity, at which point the predator opens its mouth and vigorously sucks in the prey. Moreover, we can see the five reddish prey fish of the same species forming a school in an attempt to escape from the predator while the predator is eating other prey. When the still hungry predator finally approaches the school, the little 'fugitives' scatter in terror and the school breaks into smaller schools. At the end of the animation, the satiated predator wanders away leaving one lucky survivor. Fig. 10.7 shows a still from this animation clip.

**Figures 10.7.** A large predator hunting small prey fishes while pacifist fishes, untroubled by the predator, feed on plankton

## 10.4 Animation Short: Schooling Behavior

This animation pictures a school of fish led by a larger fish that roams through the water in a zigzagging pattern. When it encounters a cylindrical obstacle, the school splits into two groups: one group consisting of a few fish passes by one side of the obstacle, while the other group comprising the remaining majority passes by the other side following the lead fish. As soon as the fish in the smaller group have cleared the obstacle they speed up to rejoin the school (see Fig. 7.15).

## 10.5 Animation Short: Mating Behavior

This animation displays courtship looping and circling, spawning ascent, and nuzzling in fish mating behaviors. The animation starts with two libidinous male poker fish (the reddish ones) swimming towards one female poker fish. When the two males encounter the female, they begin courtship looping in the hope of attracting her attention, while she hovers and bobs her head trying to decide which one to choose. The smaller male loses the competition for her attention and turns away to 'flirt' with one of the female yellow butterfly fish. The victor proudly continues his up and down looping, while in the background scene the two striped emperor angelfish have just completed their courtship circling and the female starts her spawning ascent to the surface of the water. As the camera brings us closer to the pair of angelfish, we see that the male follows the ascending female and nuzzles her abdomen as she hovers. The camera rolls back to the pair of poker fish to show the last part of their courtship circling. Upon completion of the circling, the female ascends and the male follows to nuzzle her. After three successful nudges, the mating sequence ends and the male and female part.

# 11. Conclusion and Future Work

## 11.1 Conclusion

In this dissertation we presented the results of research spanning the fields of computer graphics and artificial life. With regard to computer graphics, we have proposed, implemented, and demonstrated an animation framework that enables the creation of realistic animations of certain natural ecosystems with minimal intervention from the animator. In our approach, the virtual creatures are self-animating, as are real animals and humans. Thus, the strength of our approach to animation lies in the fact that it turns the role of the animator from that of a graphical model puppeteer to that of an virtual nature cinematographer, a job not unlike that done by nature cinematographers of the National Geographic Society. Our artificial life approach has advanced the state-of-the-art of computer animation, as evidenced by the unprecedented complexity and realism of the behavioral animations that we have been able to achieve without keyframing. With regard to artificial life, we have successfully modeled complete animals of nontrivial complexity. The convincing simulation results validate our computational models, which capture the essential features of all biological animals – biomechanics, locomotion, perception, and behavior.

In particular, we have developed a physics-based, virtual marine world inhabited by life-like artificial life forms that emulate the appearance, motion, and behavior of fishes in their natural habitats. Each artificial fish is an autonomous agent with a deformable body actuated by internal muscles, with eyes, and with a brain that includes behavior, perception and motor centers. Through controlled muscle actions, artificial fishes are able to swim through simulated water in accordance with simplified hydrodynamics. Their functional fins enable them to locomote, maintain balance, and maneuver in the water. Though rudimentary compared to real animals, their brains are nonetheless able to capture many of the most important characteristics of animal behavior and carry out perceptually guided motor tasks. In accordance with their perception of the virtual world and their internal desires, their brains arbitrate a repertoire of behaviors and subsequently select appropriate actions. The piscine behaviors the fishes exhibit include collision avoidance, foraging, preying, fleeing, schooling, and mating. The easy extensibility of our approach to the modeling of additional behaviors is suggested most evidently by the complex patterns of mating behavior that we have been able to emulate in artificial fishes.

With regard to the implementation, we have pursued a bottom-up, compositional approach in which we started by modeling the basic physics of the animal and its environment. Upon the simulated physics substrate, we effectively modeled the animal's means of locomotion. This in turn positioned us to model the animal's perceptual awareness of its world, its motivation, and last but not least, its behavior. The compositional nature of our approach to synthesizing artificial fishes was proven crucial to achieving realism. Partial solutions that do not adequately model physics, locomotion, perception, motivation and behavior, and do not combine these models intimately within the agent will not produce convincing results.

In addition to realism, computational efficiency has been one of the most important design criteria of our implementation. The fidelity of our models was carefully chosen to achieve satisfactory computational efficiency. We have strived successfully to achieve visually convincing animations with low computational cost. Using a Silicon Graphics R4400 Indigo$^2$ Extreme workstation, a simulation of ten artificial fishes, fifteen food particles and four static obstacles can run at about 4 frames/sec, including wireframe rendering time and user interface running time. With a *Reality Engine*$^2$ graphics board on the Silicon Graphics ONYX workstation, the same simulation with hardware-supported GL, fully texture mapped surface rendering runs at about 3 frames/sec. Considering the complexity of the animations, the simulation speed we have been able to achieve is more than satisfactory. The main tradeoffs that we have made in order to gain high simulation speed is the simplification of the virtual environment and the algorithms used for simulating the fish's perceptual capability.

## 11.2 Additional Impact in Animation and Artificial Life

The work reported in this dissertation has promoted further research on automatic motion synthesis for computer animation and on locomotion learning for artificial life. Grzeszczuk and Terzopoulos [33, 37] have developed a learning technique that automatically synthesizes realistic locomotion for physics-based models of animals. This technique specifically addresses animals with highly flexible and muscular bodies, such as fish, rays, dolphins, and snakes. In particular, they have established an optimization-based, multi-level learning process on top of the motor system of the artificial fish. This process forms an additional "locomotion learning" center in the artificial fish's brain (see Fig. 11.1). This center automatically learns effective motor controllers for the artificial fish biomechanical model, and abstracts them into suitably parameterized form. On the one hand, the learning center enhances the functionality of our animation system by subsuming the original laborious hand-crafting of motor controllers. On the other hand, equipped with the locomotion learning ability, the artificial fish has now 'evolved' into a more complete artificial life form.

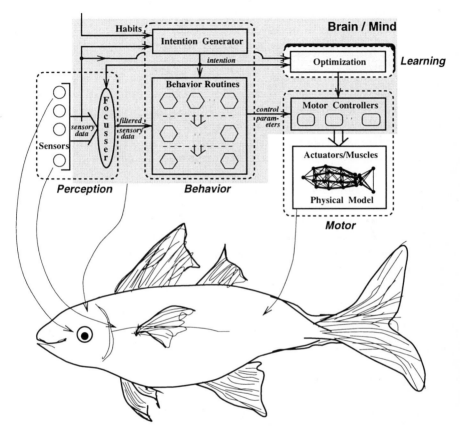

**Figures 11.1.** Locomotion learning center in the brain of the artificial fish

The ability to learn also leads to the possibility of automatically generating simple sensorimotor tasks for artificial animals, such as the fish. First steps along these lines have already been made: Greszczuk and Terzopoulos [37] imbue the artificial fish with the ability to learn to maneuver and reach a visible target. This is done by enabling the animals to learn to put into practice the compact, efficient controllers that they have previously learned. In this way, Grzeszczuk and Terzopoulos have developed dolphin models that can learn to perform a variety of "SeaWorld stunts".

## 11.3 Impact in Computer Vision and Robotics

Our work opens up several exciting avenues of research in related fields. For example, the software that we have developed has made possible interesting new approaches to computer vision and robotics.

Clearly the artificial fish is a situated virtual robot that offers a much broader range of perceptual and animate capabilities, lower cost, and higher reliability than can be expected from present-day physical robots like those described in [98]. For at least these reasons, artificial fishes in their dynamic world can serve as a proving ground for theories that profess competence at effectively linking perception to action [124]. To date, this thesis work has formed the basis for computer vision research – an approach termed *animat vision* that has been pioneered by Terzopoulos [34, 41, 35].

The animat vision methodology employs artificial animals or animats as realistic, active observers of their dynamic world. This approach can potentially liberate a significant segment of the computer vision research community from their dependence on expensive robot hardware. It addresses the needs of scientists who are motivated to understand and ultimately reverse engineer the powerful vision systems found in higher animals. As is argued by Terzopoulos [41],

> *Readily available hardware systems are terrible models of biological animals. For lack of a better alternative, however, [vision scientists] have been struggling with inappropriate hardware in their ambition to understand the complex sensorimotor functions of real animals. Moreover, their mobile robots typically lack the compute power necessary to achieve real-time response within a fully dynamic world while permitting active vision research of much significance.*

The artificial fishes and their habitats that we have developed are rich enough for grounding biologically inspired active vision systems as is shown by Terzopoulos and Rabie [34]. They have enabled active vision algorithms to be implemented entirely in software, thus circumventing the problems of hardware vision.

## 11.4 Potential Applications in Ethology

A picture is worth a thousand words...

Ethologists have long hoped to simulate animals in computers in order to facilitate the systematic study of animal behavior. As early as the seventies, ethologists Rémy and Bernadette Chauvin expressed their keen interest in such an approach to the analysis of animal behavior [116]. More recently, McFarland [125] and Roiblat [121] also emphasized the importance of such an approach:

"It is possible that ethologists will profit to a greater extent from the possibilities offered by simulation models... The availability of simulation programs makes it possible to identify which instructions devolve from a purely ethological interpretation and which from a cognitive one. A comparison of the program's behavior with the behavior actually displayed by the animal should enable the validity of the corresponding interpretation to be assessed." [121]

To this end, our artificial fish can act as a prototype model animal that provides a novel and potentially useful investigative tool. Although in several ways crude at this stage, our model can be furnished with more sophisticated behavioral mechanisms, more elaborate muscle models, etc.

Prior simulation models only allowed the modeling of one aspect of the problem to be investigated in isolation. Our model of artificial animals exemplifies a unified and complete system that allows a whole animal to be studied, from the biomechanical motor system to the perception-driven behavior system within a physics-based virtual world. In this way our approach allows the investigation of complex interactions between these different levels.

Moreover, the results of our simulation are displayed in a convenient and easy to interpret form. In effect what we have produced can be viewed as a sophisticated scientific visualization tool for ethologists that may enable new insights to be gleaned and new relationships discovered. Our work demonstrates the potential of realistic computer animation in applications to ethology.

## 11.5  Other Artificial Animals

The title of this dissertation emphasizes the generality of our artificial animal approach to computer animation, rather than its specific application in this thesis to fishes. The main components of our approach – modeling form and appearance, biomechanics, locomotion, perception, and behavior – carry over to the realistic modeling of other animals, although the details of each of these components may, to one degree or another, be animal specific. Consider, for example, the design of a realistic artificial cat.

– It is important to capture natural feline form and appearance, but clearly cats and fish differ dramatically, so different 3D models and textures would be needed to model a cat.
– Cat biomechanics obey Newton's laws of motion, as do fish biomechanics. Quite unlike the highly deformable fish body, however, an artificial cat would require the biomechanical modeling of an articulated skeleton actuated by skeletal muscles.
– With regard to locomotion, there are obvious differences between the hydrodynamic swimming of the fish and the natural quadrupedal gait of the

cat that exploits gravity and friction due to foot-ground contact. Nevertheless, for both the fish and the cat, it is crucial to the design of the higher level behavioral modeling to abstract the locomotion ability of the animal into a set of parameterized motor controllers.

- Perceptual modeling is essential in both the cat and the fish. The perception model that we have developed can with slight modification emulate the basic visual capabilities of a cat, but one may also wish to model the auditory capability of cats.
- The artificial cat requires a behavior system at least as sophisticated at the one for the artificial fish, including habits, mental state, an intention generator and behavior routines. Certain innate characteristics, such as gender, mental variables, such as hunger, and behaviors, such as collision avoidance, are common to both fish and cats, but behaviors such as scratching in the litterbox are feline specific and would require the implementation of specific behavior routines. However, the structure of our behavior control scheme remains appropriate.

To develop more complex artificial animals patterned after humans and other primates that have sophisticated intelligent behaviors, our approach can serve in the development of a reactive behavioral substrate that supports a higher-level reasoning system.

## 11.6 Future Research Directions

### 11.6.1 Animation

The behavioral animation system that we have proposed and demonstrated can be improved and further developed in many aspects. We are interested in exploring future research in a number of directions.

**Physics-based Motor Control.** Physics-based modeling offers many advantages and has, in our case, proven to be successful in generating realistic motions of fishes. However, the associated control problem for more complicated creatures remains a difficult endeavor. We would like to explore ways of simplifying the control problem, perhaps by exploiting analytical solutions to the given physical system.

**Better Hydrodynamics and a Greater Variety of Marine Animals.** In the current implementation of the artificial fish system, we model only simplified hydrodynamics in the virtual environment. An interesting future research direction would be to establish more sophisticated models of hydrodynamics. This would allow us to further examine the complex interactions between the characteristics of such a hydrodynamic environment and the motion and behavior of the artificial fishes. Furthermore, we want to implement more marine animals to enhance our virtual undersea world, such as eels, seahorses and jellyfish, etc.

**More Elaborate Perception Model.** As we have mentioned in Chapter 6, we would like to develop more sophisticated algorithms for modeling artificial animal's perception in more complex virtual environment. We are also interested in synthesizing various elaborate sensing abilities of animals, for instance, modeling diffusion for olfactory sensing.

**Modeling Emotion for Behavior Control.** Emotion is an important factor of animal behavior. It plays an essential role in describing the 'personalities' of an animal. Unlike habits, the emotion of an animal is typically associated with one or more specific objects, rather than with some generic condition. The involvement of emotion may often cause an animal to exhibit 'unusual' behavior. For example, although is generally friendly to humans, a cat may dislike a particular person and react strongly against him/her. We would like to incorporate a model of emotion into our behavior control scheme to enhance the behavior realism of the animals being animated. This model will allow additional differentiation between characters in an animation as well as offering additional high-level means of controlling their behavior.

**Higher Directability.** Last but not least, we would like to explore an intuitive way of directing the autonomous artificial creatures to a high degree. In the current implementation, it is easiest to create animations in which we do not demand highly specific control over what the creatures do and when they do it, as long as they behave naturally. However, it is not unusual to want to create an animation which shows, say, two or more events happening at roughly the same time and place. For example, when making the animation "The Undersea World of Jack Cousto" [26], we wanted to show, in a period of less than one minute of animation, two fishes displaying mating rituals while a large school of fish passes by in the background stalked by a predator shark. The most difficult part of achieving this sort of scenario is to roughly synchronize the mating, the schooling and the preying and to make schooling/preying happen in roughly the right place (the background).[1]

To achieve these sorts of synchronizations, the animator would have to spend a fair amount of time performing multiple trials, tuning the relevant parameters until the desired action sequence is achieved. An obvious way of simplifying the problem is to suspend the forward simulation of the school of fish and the shark and run a trial simulation to determine the time at which the mating occurs. Once this is known, we can start simulating the school of fish and the shark roughly around the same time. Of course, we may still need to influence the path of the school which is done by scripting the path of the 'lead' fish. Currently, these detailed manipulations are done by hand and hence may be cumbersome.

It may be possible, however, to build a higher level controller on top of the animation system we currently have in order to accomplish similar tasks

---

[1] It is easy to let the mating happen early into the animation by setting the libido parameter of the two fishes high enough.

in a much more convenient way. A promising approach for accomplishing this level of control would be employ some descriptive language for monitoring the animation process and exerting direct control over the various aspects of the simulation; e.g. the start time of some specific creatures and their paths, etc. Therefore, one of the future research directions could be to define and develop such a language and its interface to the current animation system. Blumberg and Galyean [119] recently proposed and implemented a system that addresses interactive "directability" of animated autonomous creatures. Their work marked a first step towards the aforementioned future research direction.

### 11.6.2 Artificial Life

The long-term goal of our research in the regard of artificial life is a computational theory that can, potentially, account for the interplay of locomotion, perception and behavior in higher animals. We believe that a good touchstone of such a theory is its ability to produce visually convincing results in the form of realistic computer graphics animations with little or no animator intervention.[2]

An obvious research direction would address the goals of researchers interested in evolving artificial life. We may be within reach of computational models that can imitate the spawning behaviors of the female fish and fertilization by the male. Through simulated sexual reproduction in a competitive world, gametes representing artificial fish genotypes can be fused to evolve new varieties of artificial fishes. Interestingly, Pokhilko, Pajitnov, *et al.*, have already demonstrated the simulated breeding of fish models much simpler than ours using genetic algorithms, and this idea has resulted in the fascinating computer game program "El-Fish" [122].

---

[2] In the context of artificial life there are no constraints on what should happen when.

# 12. Epilogue

The dissertation upon which this book is based was completed in 1995. Efforts toward more capable autonomous virtual characters have continued in the interim. Recent research on this topic has addressed several of the issues discussed in Chapter 10. Especially worthy of attention are two recent doctoral dissertations, the first from the Massachusetts Institute of Technology, authored by Bruce Blumberg [127], and the second from the University of Toronto, authored by John Funge [128]. The research efforts documented by these dissertations have advanced behavioral animation and artificial life to an exciting new level.

The dissertation by Blumberg, *Old Tricks, New Dogs: Ethology and Interactive Creatures*, identified and addressed five key issues in building autonomous animated characters. In the author's own words, these issues are: "Relevance (i.e. do the right things), Persistence (i.e. show the right amount of persistence), Adaptation (i.e. learn new strategies to satisfy goals), Intentionality and Motivational State (i.e. convey intentionality and motivational state in ways we intuitively understand), and External Control (i.e. allow an external entity to provide real time control at multiple levels of abstraction)." Blumberg demonstrated his computational framework by creating the virtual animated dog "Silas", among other creatures. Like the approach that we have presented in this volume, the behavioral control schemes used in Silas also draw upon research in Ethology. Blumberg's ethologically inspired model of learning is especially interesting. Using a learning algorithm that is based on a temporal difference reinforcement learning model proposed by Sutton and Barto [129], Silas can learn various associations between, say, a context and an outcome or a behavior and an outcome. Another interesting focus of Blumberg's work is the multi-level, real-time control of behavior. Unlike our biomechanically controlled fish, the low-level motions of his creatures are controlled kinematically for simplicity and speed at the expense of realism. Enabling real-time, interactive control at multiple levels of abstraction affords greater ease in the development and direction of autonomous creatures in highly interactive applications, such as immersive story-telling environments, interactive games, and smart avatars in cyberspace (see below).

The dissertation of Funge entitled *Making Them Behave: Cognitive Models for Computer Animation*, and his closely related new book *AI for Games and Animation: A Cognitive Modeling Approach* [32], tackle the high-level direction of autonomous characters from a different angle, by modeling the cognitive abilities (or intelligence) [128, 31]. Cognitive modeling is a provocative new paradigm that paves the way towards intelligent graphical characters for widespread use in the interactive game, multimedia, virtual reality, and production animation industries. Funge extends hardcore artificial intelligence methodologies and adapts them to the creation of unprecedentedly smart autonomous agents inhabiting highly kinetic virtual worlds. The approach offers a systematic technology for creating cognitively empowered self-animating characters that possess essential 'animal logic' and may be directed more like human actors.

Cognitive models go beyond behavioral models in that they govern what a character knows about its world, and how the knowledge can be used to reason and plan actions. As a computational model of cognition, Funge introduced the Cognitive Modeling Language, CML.[1] CML is based on a rigorous logical formalism from the field of artificial intelligence known as the situation calculus. CML facilitates the task of providing characters with knowledge so they can reason about their world. Knowledge is represented in CML by situations. Each situation is a snapshot of the state of the character and its world. The formalism includes possible actions that the character can perform in the current state and the expected effects of these actions. The character can use logic to reason about situation transitions or changes in its world. Analogous to the way in which a film director directs an intelligent human actor, the user can direct cognitively enabled autonomous characters by giving them behavior outlines or "loose scripts". The character uses its reasoning ability to automatically plan the appropriate behavior and fill in the missing details of the required action. The control semantics in CML are much more powerful and succinct than those commonly found in conventional imperative programming languages. Using CML, the user can specify loose, high-level scripts, or more detailed scripts, down to the explicit specification of action sequences [31].

Once characters are given the capacity to reason for themselves, the animator may specify individual character behaviors or a complete animation sequence with a brief description. Funge demonstrated a merman (fabled creature of the sea with the head and upper body of a man and the tail of a fish) that is smart enough to survive in shark-infested waters. "Duffy" the merman (Fig. 12.1) has a lower body derived from our biomechanical fish model and an anthropomorphic upper body with kinematically controlled arms. Built on top of the reactive behavior model of our fishes, Duffy swims using motor controllers similar to those for the fishes. However, unlike the predator sharks and other fishes, however, Duffy also possesses a cognitive model as described above that endows him with the ability to reason about the consequences of his actions within his physics-based virtual world.

---

[1] In his dissertation [128], Funge originally referred to CML as CLog.

Duffy's cognitive model also enables him to satisfy high-level animator-specified instructions. For example, an elaborate animation was specified by simply giving Duffy the instructions: *Try to hide when threatened by predator(s); Otherwise, try to visit potential hiding places that have not yet been visited.* In the resulting animation, when Duffy is pursued by a predator shark, "Jaws", he quickly swims for shelter towards a large, nearby rock in the undersea habitat. The shark follows to search for Duffy around the rock, but Duffy manages to evade the shark by circling the rock to remain hidden from the predator. When the shark finally loses interest and wanders away, Duffy makes a break for a larger rock. The shark spots Duffy and there ensues another round of hot pursuit with the faster-swimming predator gaining on its merman prey. Finally, Duffy is able to escape by slipping through a narrow crack in the rock through which the larger shark cannot swim. Without high-level cognitive modeling, an animation of this complexity would require several pages of C or C++ code to specify. Funge demonstrated other animations, including kinematically controlled agents that can find their way through mazes, and an intelligent camera which applies knowledge about cinematography to control shots automatically for given animation sequences.

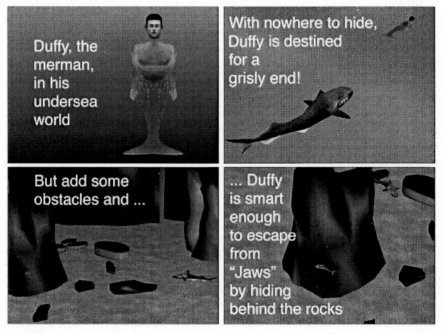

**Figures 12.1.** Cognitive modeling enables Duffy the merman to evade predator sharks (from [31]). See the original color image in Appendix D

Other dissertations recently completed at the University of Toronto have also employed our artificial fishes software to investigate important issues that are outside the scope of this book. The thesis by Yu [33] develops a "synthetic motion capture" procedure which enables a real-time version of our virtual marine world. This procedure works by replacing slow biomechanical models with fast kinematic replicas that reproduce the locomotion abilities of the original models with reasonable fidelity. Synthetic motion capture in conjunction with level-of-detail geometric modeling and occlusion culling has transformed our off-line animation of artificial fishes into an interactive, stereoscopic, virtual undersea experience in a virtual reality theater featuring a large, panoramic display [30]. The dissertations by Grzeszczuk [40, 39] investigate issues related to the learning of locomotion in artificial animals. In Chapter 11, we discussed his MS thesis work [38] on learning motor controllers in biomechanical models of animals that produce realistic locomotion and accomplish more complex motor tasks. In his PhD work [41], Grzeszczuk proposes the NeuroAnimator, a neural network technique for generating physically realistic animation. NeuroAnimators are automatically trained off-line to emulate physical dynamics by observing physics-based models in action. The NeuroAnimator approach leads to a remarkably fast algorithm for learning controllers that enable either physics-based models or their neural network emulators to synthesize motions satisfying prescribed animation goals. The method was applied successfully to learn locomotion in a biomechanically modeled dolphin based on our fish biomechanical model. The thesis by Rabie [37] employs artificial fishes to develop "animat vision", a new research paradigm in the field of computer vision which prescribes artificial animals situated in physics-based virtual worlds as autonomous virtual agents with active perception systems. The agents include foveated virtual eyes with directable gaze. Their perception relies on computer vision algorithms to analyze the retinal image streams. Equipped with animat vision, artificial fishes are capable of spatially nonuniform retinal imaging, foveation, retinal image stabilization, color object recognition, and perceptually-guided navigation [36].

Autonomous graphical characters are beginning to make their way out of the research labs and onto the internet. People are now frequenting 3D digital worlds in "cyberspace", *AlphaWorld* being the prototypical example [130].[2] AlphaWorld is accessible via the internet and visitors can use simple graphical tools to construct virtual buildings and other structures, thereby becoming "property-owning citizens". Visitors and citizens of AlphaWorld can choose or design "avatars" to represent themselves in cyberspace. Typical avatars are 3D animated anthropomorphic figures. Controlled by their human owners, avatars can roam around the virtual cities and villages and interact with one other by gesturing, chatting, etc. They can attend social activities, such as conferences in virtual convention centers, or weddings in virtual churches.

---

[2] see http://www.digitalspace.com/avatars

Current avatars are still rudimentary in their appearance and behavioral complexity. However, as the internet offers increasingly high performance, we anticipate a dramatic improvement in avatars. The techniques that we have developed in this book promise to become important in this endeavor.

Autonomous graphical characters are also beginning to impact upon the computer game industry. Behavior models have been incorporated into the new generation of game authoring (or content creation) tools that enable the development of game characters with rich behaviors at a much higher level of abstraction than is afforded by traditional game authoring tools. An example is Motivate$^{TM}$ marketed by the Motion Factory Inc.[3] Motivate comprises a suite of tools for rapidly developing 3D interactive game content. At its core is a behavior editor that combines a hierarchical finite state machine (HFSM) game logic representation with a JavaScript-like scripting language called Piccolo. The graphical character can be instructed with a script of high level commands, such as "Go there" or "Pickup that cup". The character can automatically "interpret" its script and act accordingly using a real-time motion synthesis capability, interacting with other characters and reacting to changes in the environment.

Games based on artificial life technology have become popular. *Creatures*, developed by CyberLife Technology Ltd. in Cambridge, England, is the first artificial life game title to captivate millions of people worldwide.[4] Creatures provides artificial pets called "Norns". These cute imaginary beings live in a virtual world called Albia. Norns are hatched from eggs and, like real animals, they are unique and develop their own personality as they go through their life cycle. Their characteristics are determined by simulated genetics and chemical metabolism, and their neural network-based brains can learn. Like caring for young pets, human owners observe and respond to the needs of their growing Norns. They teach Norns to eat, sleep, play, talk, explore, and eventually to reproduce.

In conclusion, the body of research and applications in advanced behavioral animation has been growing rapidly, making it impossible to cover all of the exciting new developments in this field within a few pages. However, our glimpse at the state of the art in academia and industry makes this much clear: Behavioral modeling and animation technology will continue to play a vital role as our natural world is reflected with increasing fidelity in virtual environments inhabited by synthetic characters.

*Xiaoyuan Tu*
*Research Scientist*
*Intel Corporation*
*Santa Clara, California*
*March, 1999*

---

[3] See http://www.motion-factory.com
[4] See http://creatures.mindscape.com

# A. Deformable Contour Models

A "snake" [106] is a dynamic deformable contour in the x-y image plane. We define a discrete deformable contour as $n$ equally-spaced nodes indexed by $i = 1, ..., n$, with time varying positions $\mathbf{x}_i(t) = [x_i(t), y_i(t)]$. The deformable contour's dynamic behavior can be influenced interactively by incorporating user-specified forces (e.g. mouse forces) into its equations of motion. Such behavior is governed by the system of first-order ordinary differential equations:

$$\gamma \frac{d\mathbf{x}_i}{dt} + \alpha_i + \beta_i = \mathbf{f}_i; \qquad i = 1, ..., n, \tag{A.1}$$

where $\gamma$ is a velocity-dependent damping constant, $\alpha_i(t)$ are "tension" forces which make the deformable contour act like a series of springs that resist deformation, $\beta_i(t)$ are "rigidity" forces which make the contour act like thin wire that resists bending, and $\mathbf{f}_i(t)$ are forces in the image plane $\mathbf{f}_i^I(t)$ plus the simulated mouse forces applied to the contour.

A $m \times n$ deformable mesh consists of $m + n$ contours, $n$ of which run vertically, each with $m$ nodes, and $m$ of which run horizontally each with $n$ nodes. The crossing points on the deformable mesh are nodes shared by the intersecting contours.

We express $\alpha_i$, the tension forces, in terms of the deformation of the springs connecting node $i$ to its two neighboring nodes and $\beta_i$, the rigidity forces, in terms of the second order forward finite differences as follows:

$$\alpha_i = a_i e_i \mathbf{r}_i - a_{i-1} e_{i-1} \mathbf{r}_{i-1}, \tag{A.2}$$

$$\begin{aligned}
\beta_i = &\, b_{i+1}(\mathbf{x}_{i+2} - 2\mathbf{x}_{i+1} + \mathbf{x}_i) \\
&- 2b_i(\mathbf{x}_{i+1} - 2\mathbf{x}_i + \mathbf{x}_{i-1}) \\
&+ b_{i-1}(\mathbf{x}_i - 2\mathbf{x}_{i-1} + \mathbf{x}_{i-2})
\end{aligned} \tag{A.3}$$

where $a$ and $b$ are parameters, $e_i$ is the deformation of the spring connecting node $i$ to node $i + 1$ (i.e. its current length minus its rest length), and $\mathbf{r}_i$ is the unit vector from $\mathbf{x}_i$ to $\mathbf{x}_{i+1}$. Note that $\alpha_i$ and $\beta_i$ vanish in the absence of deformation and bending.

To make the outline of the fish in the image stand out, we convert the original RGB color image into a gray-scale image $I(x, y)$. The gradient of $I$, call it $P_I(x, y)$, forms a potential field whose "ravines" coincide with the dark outline of the profile of the fish. The image force field can then be expressed as the gradient of $P_I(x,y)$, i.e. $\mathbf{f}_i^I = \nabla P_I(x,y)$) such that the ravines act as attractors to deformable contours. The contours descend and stabilize at the bottoms of the nearest ravines. In order to let the ravines attract the deformable contours from some distance away, the potential function $P_I(x,y)$ is computed as follows:

$$P_I(x,y) = G_\sigma * \|\nabla I(x,y)\|,$$

where $G_\sigma *$ denotes convolution with a 2D Gaussian smoothing filter of width $\sigma$ which broadens the ravines of $\nabla I$.

Often the user may initialize the border of the deformable mesh too far from the edges of the fish body and hence the deformable contours may become attracted by nearby dark features and fail to localize the correct outline. Should this be the case, the user can apply simulated spring forces $\mathbf{f}_i^m(t)$ by using the mouse to guide a deformable contour towards the ravine of interest [106].

Another case frequently encountered is where the profile of the fish is not composed of edges that are consistently dark or consistently white. For example, in the fish image shown in Fig. 5.5(a), part of the profile that bounds the tail and the upper body is made of white edges while the lower body is demarcated from the background by dark lines. In this case if $\mathbf{f}_i^I$ is generated such that the deformable contours are attracted to dark edges then most of the profile in Fig. 5.5(a) can not be captured properly. It is hence useful to constrain certain nodes of the border contours to selected anchor points $\mathbf{c}_i$ in the image (the interface allows the user to interactively place anchor points using the mouse). The constraints prevent the deformable contours from straying far from the anchor points, regardless of the image forces and other mouse forces. This can be achieved by attaching the deformable contour nodes with springs to their corresponding anchor points:

$$\mathbf{f}_i^c = \lambda(\mathbf{c}_i - \mathbf{x}_i)$$

where $\lambda$ is the spring constant. Using this mechanism we can also effectively deal with images where the profile of the fish is obscure.

The total external force $\mathbf{f}_i$ is therefore obtained by combining the image force $\mathbf{f}_i^I$, the mouse force $\mathbf{f}_i^m$ and the constraint force $\mathbf{f}_i^c$. The deformable contour can then be simulated by integrating the system of ordinary differential equations (A.1) forward through time using an Euler integration method [104].

# B. Visualization of the Pectoral Motions

The geometric model of a pectoral fin is a five-vertex polygonal surface with one vertex, i.e. the "root", fixed at a certain control point of the NURBS surface of the display fish model. Let us denote the root vertex as $\mathbf{v}_0$ and the four other vertices, ordered clockwise, as $\mathbf{v}_1$ to $\mathbf{v}_4$ respectively (see Fig. B.1(a)). The visualization problem is then to determine the time-varying trajectories of $\mathbf{v}_i$, $i = 1, 2, 3, 4$. It is reasonable to assume constant lengths of the vectors $\mathbf{v}_{0i}$, $i = 1, 2, 3, 4$ pointing from $\mathbf{v}_0$ to the other vertices. Therefore the control problem becomes that of determining the directions of these vectors over time.

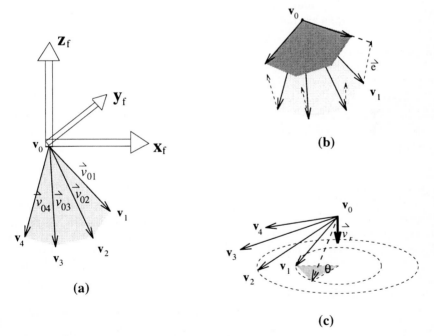

**Figures B.1.** Visualization of pectoral fin motion

Expressing vectors $\mathbf{v}_{0i}$, $i = 1, 2, 3, 4$, in the fish's local coordinate system (see Fig. 4.12) simplifies the implementation of the fin motions. Once the new positions of $\mathbf{v}_{0i}$'s are computed in the fish's local coordinate system, they are transformed back to the world coordinates system for graphics display.

## B.1 Animating the Pectoral Flapping Motion

To achieve the flapping motion, let us define displacement vectors $\mathbf{e}_i(t)$ which, when added to $\mathbf{v}_{0i}$, $i = 1, 2, 3, 4$, yield the new directions of $\mathbf{v}_{0i}$. Let the normal of the plane formed by $\mathbf{v}_{01}$ and $\mathbf{v}_{04}$ be a unit vector $\mathbf{v}_n$. The pectoral flapping motions are modeled by simply specifying the direction of the displacement vectors $\mathbf{e}_i(t)$ along $\mathbf{v}_n$ and then letting the lengths of $\mathbf{e}_i(t)$ vary over time in a sinusoidal fashion. In particular, the $\mathbf{e}_i(t)$'s are defined as follows:

$$\mathbf{e}_1(t) = a \sin(bt)\mathbf{v}_n,$$

$$\mathbf{e}_i(t) = \frac{\| \mathbf{v}_{0i} \|}{\| \mathbf{v}_{01} \|} \mathbf{e}_1(t), \quad i = 2, 3, 4,$$

where $a$ and $b$ are parameters that define the amplitude and frequency of flapping, respectively; time $t$ is discrete and equals the number of animation frames. Since the $\mathbf{v}_{0i}$'s are not coplanar (they are nearly coplanar), the shape of the fins deform slightly during the flapping motion. This is not undesirable since natural pectoral fins deform constantly due to hydrodynamic forces.

In our implementation, we choose $a$ and $b$ to be nearly proportional to $|\gamma - \pi/2|$ such that the faster the fish needs to ascend or descend, the greater the amplitude and frequency with which the fins flap. Note that $a$ and $b$ are nonzero values when $\gamma = \pi/2$ so the fins are kept in motion even when the fish is not engaged in pitching, yawing, or rolling. Fig. 5.10 shows four snapshots of the flapping motion of the pectoral fins.

## B.2 Animating the Pectoral Oaring Motion

The oaring motion of the pectoral fins is most distinguishable in natural fishes with relatively large, flat bodies that do not bend as much when swimming or turning. We capture this visual detail in our artificial butterfly fish and emperor angelfish.

To achieve the oaring motion of the pectoral fins, we let $\mathbf{v}_i$, $i = 1, 2, 3, 4$ rotate about a pre-defined unit vector $\mathbf{v}_r$ such that each $\mathbf{v}_{0i}$ traces out a cone shape (see Fig. B.1(c)). The rotation is computed using unit quaternions $q = (\cos(\theta/2), \sin(\theta/2)\mathbf{v}_r)$, where $\theta$ is the rotation angle [124]. Let the initial $\mathbf{v}_{0i}$, before rotation, be denoted by $\mathbf{v}_{0i}^o$, then we can compute the new $\mathbf{v}_{0i}$ with the formula

$$(0, \mathbf{v}_{0i}) = \bar{q}(0, \mathbf{v}_{0i}^o)q$$

where $\bar{q}$ denotes the conjugate of $q$. With $\theta$ varying from 0 to $2\pi$, each $\mathbf{v}_{0i}$ sweeps a complete cone corresponding to one full stroke of rowing. The speed with which $\theta$ changes represents the speed of rowing. We choose $\theta = \beta t$ where parameter $\beta$ is proportional to the fish's swimming speed $\|\mathbf{v}\|$ thus the faster the fish swims the faster the fins beat. Note that the above $q$ defines a "forward" oaring motion towards the direction of swimming $X_f$. To obtain a backward oaring motion, we can simply let $q = (\cos(\theta/2), -\sin(\theta/2)\mathbf{v}_r)$.

In our animations, when a butterfly fish or an emperor angelfish turns, one of the pectoral fins rows forward and the other backward as is observed in many natural, flat-body fishes. The backward oaring motions of both fins are useful when an artificial fish brakes and retreats. Fig. 5.11 shows snapshots of a butterfly fish with its forward oaring pectoral fins.

# C. Prior Action Selection Mechanisms

## C.1 Behavior Choice Network

Maes [89, 82] proposed a distributed, non-hierarchical mechanism which takes into account both internal and external stimuli in making behavioral choices. The nodes of the network represent behavior units and are connected by special purpose links, such as inhibitory links. The overall behavior of the network is an emergent property of interactions among the nodes, and of interactions between the nodes and the environment. More specifically, activation energy flows from both external sensory readings and internal motivations to different behavioral components. Different components use the links of the network to excite and inhibit each other. After some time, the activation energy accumulates in the component that represents the "best" choice, which is taken as the winner, given the current situation and motivational state of an agent. This mechanism was originally used, and proven successful, in solving relatively simple problems in a traditional AI setting (i.e. blocks world), such as choosing actions in a correct sequence so as to sand a board or spray paint a block [89]. By incorporating some biological aspects into the mechanism, it is able to deal with more complex action selection problems [82].

The main advantages of Maes' action selection mechanism are: first, the activation energy is a continuous flow which allows smooth transition from behavior to behavior; second, it is more flexible and reactive as opposed to being centrally controlled; finally, the distributed structure makes the action selection process more robust.

Some limitations have also been pointed out by Maes herself and others [91, 116]. For example, it is not clear how to achieve global functionality using this mechanism and careful tuning of parameters is needed. However, this is common to practically all distributed architectures and is not unique to this work. Also, since sensory inputs of each node are in the form of binary predicates, potentially useful information may be discarded. Moreover, Tyrrell [88] has made a critical investigation of the strictly non-hierarchical and distributed computational structure used by Maes. It is believed that the underlying structure for action selection, as suggested by ethologists, is intrinsically hierarchical, rather than "flatly" distributed. It is argued that some of the computational deficiencies due to the non-hierarchical structure of Maes' mechanism indicate that it is not well able to deal with animal-like action selection problems [88].

## C.2 Free-Flow Hierarchy

In order to allow the combining of evidence from different behavioral candidates and the selection of compromised actions, roboticists Rosenblatt and Payton [93] proposed an alternative action selection process. In their mechanism, all behavior nodes express *preferences* for each of a set of motor actions, rather than making a decision as to which is the most suitable. The final choice is a weighted sum of all the preferences. This method was later extended by Tyrrell [92] to form what is known as *free-flow* hierarchies. A free-flow hierarchy implements Rosenblatt and Payton's selection process within a hierarchical action selection architecture like that of Tinbergen [94]. All nodes in the hierarchy can influence the subsequent behavior of the agent. Activities express weighted preferences for activities lower in the hierarchy. This process propagates throughout the whole hierarchy, and as a result, instead of making a decision at each layer, a decision is only made at the lowest (i.e. action) level when the most highly preferred motor action is chosen.

Simulation results [88] show that the free-flow hierarchy outperforms Maes' mechanism and several other mechanisms. However, as Blumberg [116] points out, the relatively better performance of free-flow hierarchies may be gained at the expense of high complexity and low efficiency. This is because no focus of attention is employed in a free-flow hierarchy, and preferences need to be carefully weighted. In particular, real-time solutions may not be possible since decisions can only be made after all sensory information is processed and preferences from all components are calculated. Furthermore, all hierarchical structures suffer from a lack of flexibility in the sense that connections between components, i.e. precedences, cannot be easily altered. Free-flow hierarchies are no exception.

# D. Color Images

**Figures D.1.** Artificial fishes in their physics-based world.

**Figures D.2.** Mating behavior. Female (top) is courted by larger male.

**Figures D.3.** Predator shark stalking school of prey fish.

**Figures D.4.** Fisheye view of the world showing fishing line.

**Figures D.5.** A peaceful marine world.

**Figures D.6.** The smell of danger.

**Figures D.7.** A hapless fish is caught and pulled to the surface.

**Figures D.8.** A school of fleeing prey.

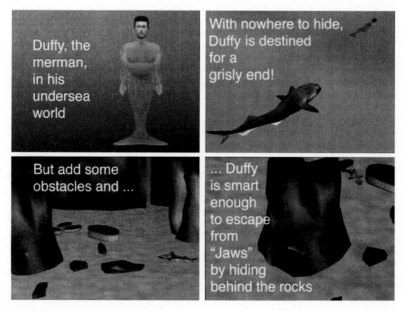

**Figures D.9.** Duffy the merman evades the shark using his coginitive abilities.

# References

1. Lasseter, J. (1987): Principles of Traditional Animation Applied to 3D Computer Animation. Proc. SIGGRAPH '87, ACM Computer Graphics, vol. 21, 35-44
2. Magnenat-Thalmann, N., Thalmann, D. (1990): Computer Animation Theory and Practice. Computer Science Workbench Series, Springer-Verlag, 2nd edition
3. Hodgins, J.K., Sweeney, P.K., Lawrence, D.G. (1992): Generating Natural-looking Motion for Computer Animation. Proc. Graphics Interface'92, 265-272
4. Miller, G.S.P. (1988): The Motion Dynamics of Snakes and Worms. Proc. SIGGRAPH'88, ACM Computer Graphics, vol. 22, 4, 169-177
5. Girard, M. (1991): Constrained Optimization of Articulated Animal Movement in Computer Animation. In *Making Them Move*. Morgan Kaufmann (Editors: Badler, N., Barsky, B., Zeltzer, D.)
6. Witkin, A., Kass, M. (1988): Spacetime Constraints. Proc. SIGGRAPH'88, ACM Computer Graphics, vol. 22, 4, 159-168
7. van de Panne, M., Fiume, E. (1993): Sensor-Actuator Networks. Proc. SIGGRAPH'93, ACM Computer Graphics
8. Ngo, J.T., Marks, J. (1993): Spacetime Constraints Revisited. Proc. SIGGRAPH'93, ACM Computer Graphics, 343-350
9. Reynolds, C. (1987): Flocks, Herds, and Schools: A Distributed Behavioral Model. Proc. SIGGRAPH'87, ACM Computer Graphics, vol. 21, 4, 25-34
10. Levy, S. (1992): *Artificial Life*. Vintage Books, New York, NY
11. Meyer, J-A., Guillot, A. (1990): Simulation of adaptive behavior in animats: Review and prospect. Proc. First International Conference on Simulation of Adaptive Behavior (From Animals to Animats). The MIT Press, Cambridge, MA (Editors: Meyer, J-A., Wilson, S.)
12. Cliff, D., Husbands, P., Meyer, J-A., Wilson. S. (Edited) (1994): From Animals to Animats: The Third International Conference on Simulation of Adaptive Behavior. The MIT Press, Cambridge, MA
13. Langton, C.G. (Edited) (1989): Artificial Life: The proceedings of an interdisciplinary workshop on the synthesis and simulation of living systems. vol. VI. Addison-Wesley
14. Beer, R. (1990): *Intelligence as Adaptive Behavior*. Academic press, New York, NY
15. Deneubourg, J.L., Franks, N., Sendova-Franks, A., Detrain, C., Chretien, L. (1990): The Dynamics of Collective Sorting Robot-like Ants and Ant-like Robots. Proc. First International conference on Simulation of Adaptive Behavior (From Animals to Animats). The MIT Press, Cambridge, MA. 356-363. (Editors: Meyer, J-A., Wilson, S.)
16. Manning, A. (1979): *An Introduction to Animal Behavior*. Addison-Wesley, 3rd edition

17. McFarland, D. (1971): *Feedback Mechanisms in Animal Behaviour*. London Academic Press, London, England

18. Terzopoulos, D., Maes, P., Prusinkiewicz, P., Reynolds, C., Sims, K., Thalmann, D. (1995): Artificial Life for Graphics, Animation, and Virtual Reality. ACM SIGGRAPH'95 Course Notes Vol. 7

19. Calvert, T.W., Chapman, J., Patla, A. (1980): The integration of subjective and objective data in the animation of human movement. Proc. SIGGRAPH '80, ACM Computer Graphics, vol. 14, 198-203

20. Varela, F.J., Bourgine, P. (Edited) (1991): The First European Conference on Artificial Life. The MIT Press, Cambridge, MA

21. Armstrong, W., Green, M. (1985): The dynamics of articulated rigid bodies for purposes of animation. J. The Visual Computer, vol. 1, **4**, 231-240

22. Wilhelms, J. (1987): Using Dynamic Analysis for Realistic animation of articulated bodies. J. IEEE Computer Graphics & Applications, vol. 7, **6**, 12-27

23. Terzopoulos, D., Platt, J., Barr, A., Fleischer, K. (1987): Elastically Deformable Models. Proc. SIGGRAPH'87, ACM Computer Graphics, vol. 21, **4**, 205-214

24. Wilson, R., Wilson, J.Q. (1985): *Watching Fishes*. Harper and Row, New York, NY

25. Tu, X., Terzopoulos, D., Fiume, E. (1993): Go Fish! SIGGRAPH Video Review Issue 91: SIGGRAPH'93 Electronic Theater

26. Tu, X., Grzeszczuk, R., Terzopoulos, D. (1995): The Undersea World of Jack Cousto. SIGGRAPH'95 Electronic Theater

27. Tu, X., Terzopoulos, D. (1994): Artificial Fishes: Physics, Locomotion, Perception, Behavior. Proc. SIGGRAPH'94, ACM Computer Graphics, 43-50

28. Tu, X., Terzopoulos, D. (1994): Perceptual modeling for the behavioral animation of fishes. Proc. Second Pacific Conference on Computer Graphics and Applications (Pacific Graphics '94), 185-200

29. Terzopoulos, D., Tu, X., Grzeszczuk, R. (1994): Artificial Fishes with Autonomous Locomotion, Perception, Behavior, and Learning in a Simulated Physical World. Artificial Life IV: Proc. Fourth International Workshop on the Synthesis and Simulation of Living Systems. The MIT Press, Cambridge, MA. 17-27 (Editors: Brooks, R., Maes, P.)

30. Yu, Q., Terzopoulos, D. (1998): Synthetic Motion Capture for Interactive Virtual Worlds. Proc. IEEE Computer Animation 98 Conference (CA98), Philadelphia, PA, June, 1998, 2-10

31. Funge, J., Tu, X., Terzopoulos, D. (1999): Cognitiv Modeling: Knowledge, Reasoning and Planning for Intelligent Characters. Proc. SIGGRAPH'99, ACM Computer Graphics

32. Funge, J. (1999): *AI for Games and Animation: A Cognitive Modeling Approach*. A. K. Peters, Natick, MA.

33. Yu, Q. (1998): *Synthetic Motion Capture for Interactive Virtual Worlds*. Master's thesis, Dept. of Computer Science, University of Toronto, Toronto, Canada

34. Terzopoulos, D., Tu, X., Grzeszczuk, R. (1994): Artificial Fishes with Autonomous Locomotion, Perception, Behavior, and Learning in a Simulated Physical World. J. Artificial Life, vol. 1, **4**, 327-350

35. Terzopoulos, D., Rabie, T.F. (1995): Animat vision. Proc. Fifth International Conference on Computer Vision

36. Terzopoulos, D., Rabie, T.F. (1997): Animat Vision: Active vision in artificial animals. Videre: Journal of Computer Vision Research, vol. 1, **1**, 2-19

37. Rabie, T.F. (1999): *Animat Vision: Active vision in artificial animals*. Ph.D dissertation, Dept. of Computer Science, University of Toronto, Toronto, Canada

38. Grzeszczuk, R., Terzopoulos, D. (1995): Automated Learning of Muscle-Actuated Locomotion Through Control Abstraction. Proc. SIGGRAPH'95, ACM Computer Graphics, 63-70

39. Grzeszczuk, R. (1998): *NeuroAnimator: Fast Neural Network Emulation and Control of Physics-Based Models*. Ph.D dissertation, Dept. of Computer Science, University of Toronto, Toronto, Canada

40. Grzeszczuk, R. (1995): *Automated Learning of Muscle-Actuated Locomotion Through Control Abstraction*. Master's thesis, Dept. of Computer Science, University of Toronto, Toronto, Canada

41. Grzeszczuk, R., Terzopoulos, D., Hinton, G. (1998): NeuroAnimator: Fast Neural Network Emulation and Control of Physics-Based Models. Proc. SIGGRAPH'98, ACM Computer Graphics, 9-20

42. Terzopoulos, D. (1995): Modeling Living Systems for Computer Vision. Proc. IJCAI'95, vol. 1, 1003-1013

43. Terzopoulos, D., Fleischer, K. (1988): Deformable Models. J. Visual Computer, vol. 4, **6**, 306-331

44. Witkin, A., Welch, W. (1990): Fast Animation and Control of Nonrigid Structures. Proc. SIGGRAPH'90, ACM Computer Graphics, vol. 24, **4**, 243-252

45. Barzel, R., Barr, A.H. (1988): A Modeling System Based on Dynamic Constraints. Proc. SIGGRAPH'88, ACM Computer Graphics, vol. 22, **4**, 179-188

46. Wejchert, J., Haumann, D. (1991): Animation Aerodynamics. Proc. SIGGRAPH'91, ACM Computer Graphics, vol. 25, **4** 19-22

47. Badler, N., Barsky, B., Zeltzer, D. (1991): *Making Them Move*. Morgan Kaufmann

48. Hodgins, J.K., Wooten, W.L., Brogan, D.C., O'Brien, J.F. (1995): Animating Human Athletics. Proc. SIGGRAPH'95, ACM Computer Graphics, 71-78

49. Platt, J.C., Barr, A.H. (1988): Constraint methods for flexible models. Proc. SIGGRAPH'88, ACM Computer Graphics, 279-288

50. Isaacs, P., Cohen, M. (1987): Controling Dynamic Simulation with Kinematic Constraints, Behavior Functions, and Inverse Dynamics. Proc. SIGGRAPH'87, ACM Computer Graphics, vol. 22, **4**, 215-224

51. Liu, Z., Gortler, S.J., Cohen, M.F. (1994): Hierarchical Spacetime Control. Proc. SIGGRAPH'94, ACM Computer Graphics, 35-42

52. Funge, J. (1995): Constraints and Computer Animation. Ph.D. Qualifying Exam Paper

53. Terzopoulos, D., Waters, K. (1990): Physically-based Facial Modelling, Analysis, and Animation. J. Visulization and Computer Animation, vol, 1, 73-80

54. Lee, Y., Terzopoulos, D., Waters, K. (1993) Constructing physics-based facial models of individuals. Proc. Graphics Interface'93, 1-8

55. Lee, Y., Terzopoulos, D., Waters, K. (1995): Realistic Modeling for Facial Animation. Proc. SIGGRAPH'95, ACM Computer Graphics, 55-62

56. Raibert, M.H., Hodgins, J.K. (1991): Animation of Dynamic Legged Locomotion. Proc. SIGGRAPH'91, ACM Computer Graphics, vol. 25, **4**, 349-358

57. McKenna, M., Pieper, S., Zeltzer, D. (1990): Control of a Virtual Actor: The Roach. Proc. ACM SIGGRAPH'90 Symposium on Interactive 3D Graphics, vol. 24, **2**, 165-174

58. Brooks, R.A. (1991): Intelligence without representation. J. Artificial Intelligence, **47**, 139-159

59. Stewart, A.J., Cremer, J.F. (1992): Beyond keyframing: An algorithmic approach to animation. Proc. Graphics Interface'92, 273-281

60. Alexander, R.M. (1992): *Exploring Biomechanics*. Scientific American Library, New York, NY

61. Webb, P.W. (1989): *Form and Function in Fish Swimming*. Scientific American, vol. 251, **1**
62. Blake, R.W. (1983): *Fish Locomotion*. Cambridge University Press, Cambridge, England
63. Alexander, R.M. (1982): *Locomotion of Animals*. Chapman & Hall,New York, NY
64. Pandy, M.G., Anderson, F.C., Hull, D.G. (1992): A parameter optimization approach for the optimal control of large-scale musculoskeletal systems. Trans. ASME, vol. 114, **450**
65. Sims, K. (1994): Evolving Virtual Creatures. Proc. SIGGRAPH '94, ACM Computer Graphics, 15-22
66. Reynolds, C. (1982): Computer Animation with Scripts and Actors. Proc. SIG-GRAPH'82, ACM Computer Graphics, vol. 16, **3**, 289-296
67. Zeltzer, D. (1982): Motor control techniques for figure animation. J. IEEE Computer Graphics and Application, vol. 2, **9**, 53-59
68. Wilhelms, J. (1990): Behavioral Animation Using an Interactive Network. Proc. Computer Animation'90. Springer-Verlag. 95-106 (Editors: Thalmann, N., Thalmann, D.)
69. Mataric, M.J. (1994): *Interaction and Intelligent Behavior. Ph.D Dissertation*. Department of EECS, MIT, Cambridge, MA
70. Renault, O., Magnenat-Thalmann, N., Thalmann, D. (1990): A Vision-based Approach to Behavioural Animation. J. Visualization and Computer Animation, vol. 1, 18-21
71. Thalmann, D. (1995): Virtual Sensors: A Key Tool For the Artificial Life of Virtual Actor. Proc. Third Pacific Conference on Computer Graphics and Applications (Pacific Graphics '95), J. Computer Graphics and Application. World Scientific, Singapore. 22-40 (Editors: Shin, S.Y., Kunii, T.L.)
72. Tinbergen, N. (1950): The Hierarchical Organization of Nervous Mechanisms Underlying Instinctive Behaviour. J. Symposia of the Society for Experimental Biology, vol. 4, 305-512
73. Lorenz, K.Z. (1981): *The Foundations of Ethology*. Simon and Schuster, New York, NY
74. McFarland, D. (1987): *The Oxford Companion to Animal Behaviour*. Oxford University Press, Oxford, England
75. Adler, H.E. (1975): *Fish Behavior: Why Fishes do What They Do*. T.F.H Publications, Neptune City, NJ
76. Braitenberg, V. (1984): *Vehicles, experiments in synthetic psychology*. The MIT Press, Cambridge, MA
77. Resnick, M. (1987): LEGO, Logo, and Life. Artificial Life: The proceedings of an interdisciplinary workshop on the synthesis and simulation of living systems, vol. VI, 397-406
78. Tyrrell, T. (1992): Defining the Action Selection Problem. Proc. Fourteenth Annual Conference of the Cognitive Science Society
79. McFarland, D., Sibly, R. (1975): The Behavioural Final Common Path. Philosophical Transactions of the Royal Society (Series B) **270**, 265-293
80. Dawkins, R. (1989): *The Selfish Gene*. Oxford University Press, Oxford, England, 2nd edition
81. Werner, G. (1994): Using Second Order Neural Connections for Motivation of Behavioral Choices. Proc. Third International Conference on Simulation of Adaptive Behavior (From Animals to Animats). The MIT Press, Cambridge, MA. 108-117 (Editors: Cliff, D., Husbands, P., Meyer, J-A., Wilson, S.)

82. Maes, P. (1991): A Bottom-up Mechanism for Behavior Selection in an Artificial Creature. Proc. First International Conference on Simulation and Adaptive Behavior (From Animals to Animats). The MIT Press, Cambridge, MA (Editors: Meyer, J-A., Wilson, S.)

83. Sun, H., Green, M. (1993): The Use of Relations for Motion Control in an Environment With Multiple Moving Objects. Proc. Graphics Interface'93. 209-218

84. Agre, P., Chapman, D. (1987): Pengi: An implementation of a theory of activity. Proc. AAAI. 268-272

85. Kaelbling, L. (1987): An Architecture for Intelligent Reactive Systems. Proc. 1986 Workshop: Reasoning about Actions and Plans. Morgan Kaufmann

86. Brooks, R.A. (1986): A Robust Layered Control System for a Mobile Robot. IEEE J. Robotics and Automation, vol. 1, **2**, 14-23

87. Anderson, T., Donath, M. (1990): Animal Behavior as a Paradigm for Developing Robot Autonomy. In *Robotics and Autonomous Systems*. Elservier Science Publishers B.V., North-Holland. **6**, 145-168

88. Tyrrell, T. (1993): *Computational Mechanisms for Action Selection*. Ph.D dissertation, Centre for Cognitive Science, University of Edinburgh

89. Maes, P. (1990): Situated Agents Can Have Goals. In *Designing Autonomous Agents*. The MIT Press, Cambridge, MA. 49-70

90. Beer, R., Chiel, H.J. (1991): The Neural Basis of Behavioral Choice in an Artificial Insect. Proc. First International Conference on Simulation of Adaptive Behavior (From Animals to Animats). The MIT Press, Cambridge, MA. 247-254 (Editors: Meyer, J-A., Wilson, S.)

91. Sahota, M.K. (1994): Action Selection for Robots in Dynamic Environments through Inter-behaviour Bidding. Proc. Third International Conference on Simulation of Adaptive Behavior (From Animals to Animats). The MIT Press, Cambridge, MA. 138-142 (Editors: Cliff, D., Husbands, P., Meyer, J-A., Wilson. S.)

92. Tyrrell, T. (1992): The Use of Hierarchies for Action Selection. Proc. Second International Conference on Simulation of Adaptive Behavior (From Animals to Animats). The MIT Press, Cambridge, MA. 138-146 (Editors: Meyer, J-A., Roitblat, H.L., Wilson. S.)

93. Rosenblatt, K.J., Payton, D.W. (1989): A Fine-Grained Alternative to the Subsumption Architecture for Mobile Robot Control. Proc. IEEE/INNS International Joint Conference on Neural Networks

94. Tinbergen, N. (1951): *The Study of Instinct*. The Clarendon Press, Oxford, England

95. Coderre, B. (1987): Modeling behavior in Petworld. J. Artificial Life: Proc. an Interdisciplinary Workshop on the Synthesis and Simulation of Living Systems. Vol. VI, 407-420

96. Badler, N.I., Phillips, C.W., Webber, B.L. (1993): *Simulating Humans: Computer Graphics Animation and Control*. Oxford University Press, New York, NY

97. McFarland, D. (1993): *Animal Behaviour: Psychobiology, Ethology, and Evolution*. Longman Scientific and Technical, Harlow, England, 2nd edition

98. Wilson, S. (1990): The Animat Path to AI. Proc. First International Conference on Simulation of Adaptive Behavior (From Animals to Animats). The MIT Press, Cambridge, MA. 15-21 (Editors: Meyer, J.A., Wilson, S.)

99. Maes, P. (Edited) (1991): *Designing Autonomous Agents*. The MIT Press, Cambridge, MA

100. Prince, J.H. (1981): *How Animals Move*. Elsevier/Nelson Books, New York, NY

101. Webb, P.W. (1984): Body form, locomotion and foraging in aquatic verte-brates. J. American Zoologist, vol. 24, **1**, 107-120
102. Massey, B.S. (1983): *Mechanics of Fluids*. Van Nostrand Reinhold (UK) Co. Ltd. 5th Edition
103. Bathe, K-J., Wilson, E.L. (1976): *Numerical Methods in Finite Element Analysis*. Prentice-Hall, Englewood Cliffs, NJ
104. Press, W.H., Flannery, B.P., Teukolsky, S.A., Vetterling, W.T. (1986):*Numerical Recipes: The Art of Scientific Computing*. Cambridge University Press, Cambridge, England
105. Black, R.W. (1983): Functional design and burst-and-coast swimming in fishes. Canadian J. Zoology, vol. 61, 2491-2494
106. Kass, M., Witkin, A., Terzopoulos, D. (1987): Snakes: Active Contour Models. International Journal of Computer Vision, vol. 1, **4**, 321-331
107. Carlbom, I., Terzopoulos, D., Harris, K.M. (1994): Computer-Assisted registration, segmentation, and 3D reconstruction from images of neuronal tissue sections. IEEE Trans. medical imaging, vol. 13, **2**, 351-362
108. Smythe, R.H. (1975): *Vision In The Animal World*. The Macmillan Press
109. Tansley, K. (1965): *Vision in Vertebrates*. Chapman and Hall, London, England
110. Foley, J., van Dam, A., Feiner, S., Hughes, J. (1990): *Computer Graphics Principles and Practice*. Addison-Wesley, 2nd edition
111. Tsotsos, J.K., Culhane, S.M., Wai, W., Lai, Y., Davis, N., Nuflo, F. (1995): Modeling visual attention via selective tuning. J. Artificial Intelligence
112. Barrow, H.G., Tenenbaum, J.M. (1981): Computational Vision. Proc. IEEE, vol. 69, **5**, 572-595
113. Toates, F. (1980): *Animal Behaviour: A System Approach*. John Wiley & Sons, Chichester, England
114. Dawkins, R. (1976): Hierarchical Organization: A Candidate principle for ethology. In *Growing Points in Ethology*. Cambridge University Press, Cambridge, England
115. Ludlow, A. (1980): The Evolution and Simulation of a Decision Maker. In *Analysis of Motivational Processes*. Academic Press, London, England (Editors: Toates, F., Halliday, T.)
116. Blumberg, B. (1994): Action-Selection in Hamsterdam: Lessons from Ethology. Proc. Third International Conference on Simulation of Adaptive Behavior (From Animals to Animats). The MIT Press, Cambridge, MA. 108-117 (Editors: Cliff, D., Husbands, P., Meyer, J-A., Wilson. S.)
117. Chauvin, R., Muckensturm-Chauvin, B. (1977): *Behavioral Complexity*. International University Press, New York, NY
118. Alexander, R.M. (1983): *Animal Mechanics*. Blackwell Scientific Publications, Oxford, England. 2nd Edition
119. Thresher, R.E. (1984): *Reproduction in Reef Fishes*. T.F.H. Publications, Neptune City, NJ
120. Blumberg, B.M., Galyean, T.A. (1995): Multi-Level Direction of Autonomous Creatures for Real-Time Virtual Environments. Proc. SIGGRAPH'95, ACM Computer Graphics, 47-54
121. Overmars, M. (1995): Forms Library. Department of Computer Science, Utrecht University, Utrecht, the Netherlands (Version 2.3)
122. Roiblat, H.L. (1994): Mechanism and process in animal behavior: Models of animals, animals as models. Proc. Third International Conference on Simulation of Adaptive Behavior (From Animals to Animats). The MIT Press, Cambridge, MA. 12-21 (Editor: Cliff, D., Husbands, P., Meyer, J-A., Wilson, S.)

123. Corcoran, E. (1992): One Fish, Two Fish: How to raise a school of tempting software toys, Scientific American

124. Shoemake, K. (1985): Animating Rotation with Quaternion Curves. Proc. SIGGRAPH '85 , ACM Computer Graphics, vol. 19, 245-254

125. Ballard, D. (1991): Animate Vision. J. Artificial Intelligence, **48**, 57-86

126. McFarland, D. (1993): *Intelligent Behavior in Animals and Robots.* The MIT Press, Cambridge, MA

127. Blumberg, B. (1996):*Old Tricks, New Dogs: Ethology and Interactive Creatures.* Ph.D dissertation, Dept. of Computer Science, Massachusetts Institute of Technology, Cambridge, MA

128. Funge, J. (1998): *Making Them Behave: Cognitive Models for Computer Animation.* Ph.D dissertation, Dept. of Computer Science, University of Toronto, Toronto, Canada

129. Sutton, R., Barto, A.G. (1990): Time-Derivative Models of Pavlovian Reinforcement. *Learning and Computational Neuroscience: Foundations of Adaptive Networks.* The MIT Press, Cambridge, MA. (Editors: Gabriel, M., Moore, J.)

130. Damer, B. (1997): *Avatars! : Exploring and Building Virtual Worlds on the Internet.* Peachpit Press, Berkeley, CA

# Index

# Springer
# and the
# environment

At Springer we firmly believe that an international science publisher has a special obligation to the environment, and our corporate policies consistently reflect this conviction.

We also expect our business partners – paper mills, printers, packaging manufacturers, etc. – to commit themselves to using materials and production processes that do not harm the environment. The paper in this book is made from low- or no-chlorine pulp and is acid free, in conformance with international standards for paper permanency.

# Lecture Notes in Computer Science

For information about Vols. 1–1676
please contact your bookseller or Springer-Verlag

Vol. 1711: N. Zhong, A. Skowron, S. Ohsuga (Eds.), New Directions in Rough Sets, Data Mining, and Granular-Soft Computing. Proceedings, 1999. XIV, 558 pages. 1999. (Subseries LNAI).

Vol. 1712: H. Boley, A Tight, Practical Integration of Relations and Functions. XI, 169 pages. 1999. (Subseries LNAI).

Vol. 1713: J. Jaffar (Ed.), Principles and Practice of Constraint Programming – CP'99. Proceedings, 1999. XII, 493 pages. 1999.

Vol. 1714: M.T. Pazienza (Eds.), Information Extraction. IX, 165 pages. 1999. (Subseries LNAI).

Vol. 1715: P. Perner, M. Petrou (Eds.), Machine Learning and Data Mining in Pattern Recognition. Proceedings, 1999. VIII, 217 pages. 1999. (Subseries LNAI).

Vol. 1716: K.Y. Lam, E. Okamoto, C. Xing (Eds.), Advances in Cryptology – ASIACRYPT'99. Proceedings, 1999. XI, 414 pages. 1999.

Vol. 1717: Ç. K. Koç, C. Paar (Eds.), Cryptographic Hardware and Embedded Systems. Proceedings, 1999. XI, 353 pages. 1999.

Vol. 1718: M. Diaz, P. Owezarski, P. Sénac (Eds.), Interactive Distributed Multimedia Systems and Telecommunication Services. Proceedings, 1999. XI, 386 pages. 1999.

Vol. 1719: M. Fossorier, H. Imai, S. Lin, A. Poli (Eds.), Applied Algebra, Algebraic Algorithms and Error-Correcting Codes. Proceedings, 1999. XIII, 510 pages. 1999.

Vol. 1720: O. Watanabe, T. Yokomori (Eds.), Algorithmic Learning Theory. Proceedings, 1999. XI, 365 pages. 1999. (Subseries LNAI).

Vol. 1721: S. Arikawa, K. Furukawa (Eds.), Discovery Science. Proceedings, 1999. XI, 374 pages. 1999. (Subseries LNAI).

Vol. 1722: A. Middeldorp, T. Sato (Eds.), Functional and Logic Programming. Proceedings, 1999. X, 369 pages. 1999.

Vol. 1723: R. France, B. Rumpe (Eds.), UML'99 – The Unified Modeling Language. XVII, 724 pages. 1999.

Vol. 1724: H. I. Christensen, H. Bunke, H. Noltemeier (Eds.), Sensor Based Intelligent Robots. Proceedings, 1998. VIII, 327 pages. 1999 (Subseries LNAI).

Vol. 1725: J. Pavelka, G. Tel, M. Bartošek (Eds.), SOFSEM'99: Theory and Practice of Informatics. Proceedings, 1999. XIII, 498 pages. 1999.

Vol. 1726: V. Varadharajan, Y. Mu (Eds.), Information and Communication Security. Proceedings, 1999. XI, 325 pages. 1999.

Vol. 1727: P.P. Chen, D.W. Embley, J. Kouloumdjian, S.W. Liddle, J.F. Roddick (Eds.), Advances in Conceptual Modeling. Proceedings, 1999. XI, 389 pages. 1999.

Vol. 1728: J. Akoka, M. Bouzeghoub, I. Comyn-Wattiau, E. Métais (Eds.), Conceptual Modeling – ER '99. Proceedings, 1999. XIV, 540 pages. 1999.

Vol. 1729: M. Mambo, Y. Zheng (Eds.), Information Security. Proceedings, 1999. IX, 277 pages. 1999.

Vol. 1730: M. Gelfond, N. Leone, G. Pfeifer (Eds.), Logic Programming and Nonmonotonic Reasoning. Proceedings, 1999. XI, 391 pages. 1999. (Subseries LNAI).

Vol. 1732: S. Matsuoka, R.R. Oldehoeft, M. Tholburn (Eds.), Computing in Object-Oriented Parallel Environments. Proceedings, 1999. VIII, 205 pages. 1999.

Vol. 1733: H. Nakashima, C. Zhang (Eds.), Approaches to Intelligent Agents. Proceedings, 1999. XII, 241 pages. 1999. (Subseries LNAI).

Vol. 1734: H. Hellwagner, A. Reinefeld (Eds.), SCI: Scalable Coherent Interface. XXI, 490 pages. 1999.

Vol. 1564: M. Vazirgiannis, Interactive Multimedia Documents. XIII, 161 pages. 1999.

Vol. 1591: D.J. Duke, I. Herman, M.S. Marshall, PREMO: A Framework for Multimedia Middleware. XII, 254 pages. 1999.

Vol. 1624: J. A. Padget (Ed.), Collaboration between Human and Artificial Societies. XIV, 301 pages. 1999. (Subseries LNAI).

Vol. 1635: X. Tu, Artificial Animals for Computer Animation. XIV, 172 pages. 1999.

Vol. 1646: B. Westfechtel, Models and Tools for Managing Development Processes. XIV, 418 pages. 1999.

Vol. 1735: J.W. Amtrup, Incremental Speech Translation. XV, 200 pages. 1999. (Subseries LNAI).

Vol. 1736: L. Rizzo, S. Fdida (Eds.): Networked Group Communication. Proceedings, 1999. XIII, 339 pages. 1999.

Vol. 1737: P. Agouris, A. Stefanidis (Eds.), Integrated Spatial Databases. Proceedings, 1999. X, 317 pages. 1999.

Vol. 1738: C. Pandu Rangan, V. Raman, R. Ramanujam (Eds.), Foundations of Software Technology and Theoretical Computer Science. Proceedings, 1999. XII, 452 pages. 1999.

Vol. 1740: R. Baumgart (Ed.): Secure Networking – CQRE [Secure] '99. Proceedings, 1999. IX, 261 pages. 1999.

Vol. 1741: A. Aggarwal, C. Pandu Rangan (Eds.), Algorithms and Computation. Proceedings, 1999. XIII, 448 pages. 1999.

Vol. 1742: P.S. Thiagarajan, R. Yap (Eds.), Advances in Computing Science – ASIAN'99. Proceedings, 1999. XI, 397 pages. 1999.

Vol. 1744: S. Staab, Extracting Degree Information from Texts. X; 187 pages. 1999. (Subseries LNAI).

Vol. 1745: P. Banerjee, V.K. Prasanna, B.P. Sinha (Eds.), High Performance Computing – HiPC'99. Proceedings, 1999. XXII, 412 pages. 1999.

Vol. 1746: M. Walker (Ed.), Cryptography and Coding. Proceedings, 1999. IX, 313 pages. 1999.

Vol. 1747: N. Foo (Ed.), Adavanced Topics in Artificial Intelligence. Proceedings, 1999. XV, 500 pages. 1999. (Subseries LNAI).

Vol. 1748: H.V. Leong, W.-C. Lee, B. Li, L. Yin (Eds.), Mobile Data Access. Proceedings, 1999. X, 245 pages. 1999.

Vol. 1749: L. C.-K. Hui, D.L. Lee (Eds.), Internet Applications. Proceedings, 1999. XX, 518 pages. 1999.

Vol. 1750: D.E. Knuth, MMIXware. VIII, 550 pages. 1999.